Learning to Program in Structured COBOL Part 2

by
Timothy R. Lister
and
Edward Yourdon

YOURDON Press
1133 Avenue of the Americas
New York, New York 10036

ISBN: 0-917072-03-0

DEDICATION

This book is for the women in our lives —
with special appreciation to our cleaning lady,
who for many months
recognized that the hundreds of tiny scraps of paper
represented a manuscript in progress,
rather than mere trash.

CONTENTS

ACKNOWLEDGMENTS

This book has made it into print because of the work, encouragement, and goading of many people. Wendy Eakin, Toni Nash, and all of the YOURDON Press staff did an excellent job of editing our scribbles on yellow lined paper, entering the text into the PDP-11, and, finally, moving it into book form. Rick Weiland, Martha Cichelli, and Bob Abbott, COBOL experts all, politely slashed and massaged the original text into technical accuracy; and Gabe Pham somehow managed to get the pieces of code through a COBOL compiler. Our thanks to all.

Finally, we would like to thank the hundreds of COBOL programmers who listened to our ideas, and argued with us about how best to produce COBOL programs that work. We are indebted to them for forcing us to examine the problems and the solutions.

November 1977   T.R.L.
New York, N. Y.   E.Y.

PREFACE

This book is intended for two audiences: the programmer trainee who has successfully completed *Learning to Program in Structured COBOL, Part 1* and the experienced COBOL programmer who is learning the techniques of Structured Programming. Sections of this text address specific instructions and their rules of usage and, therefore, may seem to be of little use to the experienced professional. However, we urge our audience to read the entire text, if for no other reason than to brush up on the 1974 ANS COBOL standard facilities.

We have not tried to produce a palatable reference manual for COBOL; rather, we have tried to present a text which introduces COBOL within the environment of applications development. In attempting to accomplish this goal, we occasionally have slipped into non-ANS COBOL, often into IBM-defined COBOL. This has not been done as an endorsement of any particular vendor, but only to better prepare the student for the business applications world.

8 Programming for Change

8.1 Characteristics of a good COBOL program

What are we trying to accomplish when we write a COBOL program? The most obvious answer is that we are trying to make a computer solve some well-defined problem. That is, our aim is to write a program that works according to its specifications.

That may seem like a trivial statement — *of course* our aim is to write a working program. However, it is a demanding task, and we should not underestimate the difficulty of producing a correct — demonstrably correct — program. Our orders to the computer must be exact. If we make even one error, one error in thousands of statements, the entire program may fail. A program either works, or it doesn't — programmers are rarely congratulated for almost solving a problem. So, let's keep in mind that the first and foremost characteristic of a COBOL program is, it works.

What are some other characteristics of a good COBOL program? Should it be efficient? elegant? devious? You'll find many of your colleagues striving to develop programs with these characteristics — but it's our strong feeling that the second most important characteristic of a COBOL program is its readability. We should be able to read what we write. Sooner or later, we will be asked to add a new feature to our program, or change some aspect of its operation; indeed, sooner or later, someone else will be asked to change our program — and we may not be around to answer any questions about it. In order to make the modification process easy, it is important that we — or the unfortunate maintenance programmer who has been stuck with the job of looking after our program — understand (a) *what* the code is trying to accomplish, (b) *how* the code accomplishes its purpose, and (c) *where* the alterations should go.

Thus, our COBOL program must be understandable to human beings, as well as to the computer that will execute it. Indeed, we must pay a great deal of attention to the human beings who will read our code — for they (and we) have a limited ability to understand complex, obscure, devious logic. All of the COBOL code in this book is written with the intention of being readable, as well as correct.

A third — and also very important — characteristic of all good COBOL programs is their ability to be changed easily. If the specification for the program changes in a minor way, then the changes to the actual code should be simple, localized, and limited in number. Major alterations to a program are time-consuming, costly, and error-prone, and we should be able to avoid them if we design and implement our programs properly.

Changes to computer systems will continue as long as the enterprise that uses the computer system (e.g., the business organization) continues to evolve. We don't want to treat program specifications as a never-changing oil portrait, but as a single frame of a motion picture. We want to organize our programs in such a way that we don't have to rewrite the entire program when the next frame comes into focus.

In summary, we should ask ourselves three important questions before we announce that our program is finished:

1.   Have I solved the problem defined by the specifications?

2.   Would another COBOL programmer easily understand how I have solved the problem?

3.   Can my program be modified easily when the changes come?

Unless the answer is yes to all three questions, we are not finished.

Are there other characteristics of a good COBOL program? Yes, there are at least two: It should be economical to develop, and it should be economical to operate. We find that if a program is designed for easy maintenance and modification, it is usually easy — and, therefore, economical — for the original programmer to develop. That is, the same things that will make it difficult for someone else to understand your program five years from now will make it difficult for you to understand the program while you're in the midst of coding and debugging it. Similarly, we find that attention to understandability and maintainability usually produces a reasonably efficient program, one that does not consume too much memory or too many microseconds of CPU time. It may still be possible to improve the efficiency of such a program, so we will discuss some guidelines for optimizing programs in Chapter 15.

A final comment about maintainability: Your use of the COBOL programming language goes a long way toward making a program easy to understand and easy to modify. Indeed, one of the major reasons why COBOL is the most widely used business-oriented programming language is its relative independence from specific hardware features. The American National Standards Institute (ANSI) sets standards requirements for the COBOL language, and most major computer manufacturers adhere to those standards.[1] Thus, by writing in ANSI COBOL, we should be able to run our programs on a wide range of computers. The same programs should work on Burroughs, IBM, Honeywell, and a host of other machines — a versatility that is not characteristic of several other programming languages. Thus, COBOL's popularity is strong evidence of the computer industry's desire for changeable, maintainable programs.

---

[1]Some COBOL statements are not required by ANSI, but are supplied by individual computer manufacturers as "extensions" to the language. They are probably marked in your COBOL reference manual in some special way; it is common for such nonstandard statements to be shaded in gray. You should ascertain your installation's non-ANSI COBOL statements, and determine whether they are to be used.

8.2 Hierarchies and structure charts

One of the best ways to organize flexible, maintainable systems is in a *hierarchical* fashion. All kinds of systems can be viewed as hierarchies. For example, here is a piece of the hierarchy of the animal kingdom:

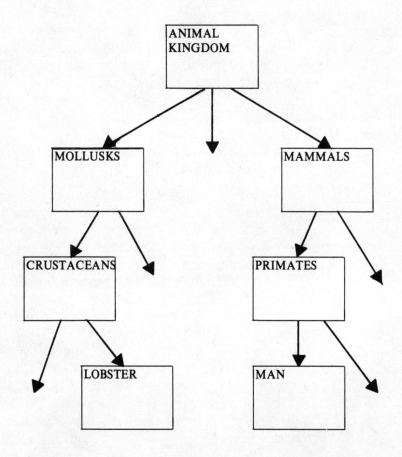

The company that you work for, or the school that you attend, is probably organized in a hierarchical fashion; there's probably a president at the top, and it's likely that you're a great deal closer to the bottom of the hierarchy than to the top.

As you will recall from Part 1 of this series,[2] we design computer programs and systems in a hierarchical fashion, and document those designs in a fashion that highlights the hierarchy. For example, here is a structure chart for a system that will write payroll checks for three types of workers:

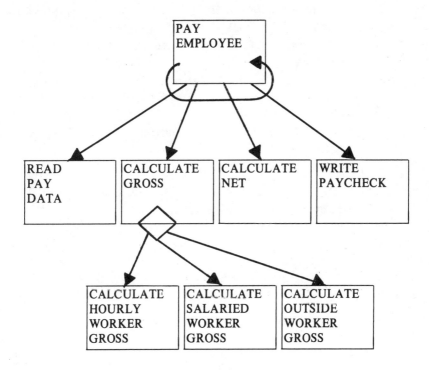

Note that the structure chart shows that there are workers who are paid on an hourly basis, other workers who are salaried, and non-regular workers who are paid on a contract basis.

---

[2]Edward Yourdon, Chris Gane, Trish Sarson, *Learning to Program in Structured COBOL, Part 1* (New York: YOURDON inc., 1976).

The boxes in the diagram on the previous page are known as modules; the arrows, which are also called connections, show the references made from one module to another. There is a one-to-one relationship between the modules in a structure chart, and groups of code in our COBOL program; indeed, every instruction in a COBOL program is a member of one, and only one, module.

The curved arrow wrapping around the connections from PAY EMPLOYEE is our notation for a loop. In this case, the chart clearly shows that PAY EMPLOYEE refers to READ PAY DATA, CALCULATE GROSS, CALCULATE NET, and WRITE PAYCHECK in a repetitive fashion, within a loop. Without this loop, the program would calculate only one employee's paycheck. Although the structure chart does not show the details of the loop, we can assume that the top-level module invokes the four second-level modules repeatedly until all of the employee paychecks have been processed.

There is another graphic convention that we should point out. The diamond at the base of CALCULATE GROSS is the symbol for a decision. It shows that CALCULATE GROSS contains some instruction, or instructions, to determine whether CALCULATE HOURLY WORKER GROSS, or CALCULATE SALARIED WORKER GROSS, or CALCULATE OUTSIDE WORKER GROSS should be invoked. We may assume that for each employee only one of the three modules will be invoked.

Typically, we read a structure chart from the top down. The topmost module is the module that begins and ends the program. Each module on the second level receives control from PAY EMPLOYEE, carries out its task, and returns control to its invoker — i.e., to PAY EMPLOYEE. These second-level modules do not return to the first executable statement in PAY EMPLOYEE, but rather to the statement immediately following the instruction that gave them control. All of the modules in the structure chart are assumed to behave in this fashion — if they did not, the structure chart would not represent a true hierarchy in the sense in which we will be using that word.

It is permissible for a module to have more than one invoker — that is, more than one "boss." For example, the structure chart below shows that CHECK FOR NUMERICS will return control to EDIT ACCOUNT NO or to EDIT ZIP CODE, depending on which of those "bosses" called it.

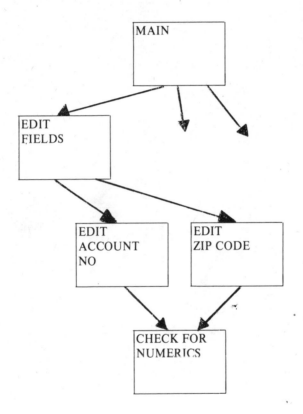

All modules and all connections between modules are shown on a structure chart, but it is not necessary to show *all* of the loops and decisions. Indeed, to show all of the loops and decisions would unnecessarily clutter most structure charts; thus, as a rule of thumb, we usually only show the most important loops and decisions on the structure chart — i.e., those that are important for an understanding of the overall program or system.

8.3 Cohesion and coupling in modular systems

How do we go about designing programs in a hierarchical fashion? Unfortunately, many programmers design in a rather haphazard manner, so they really have no idea of the kind of hierarchy that will evolve. For example, an alternative design for the payroll system we discussed in the previous section might look like this:

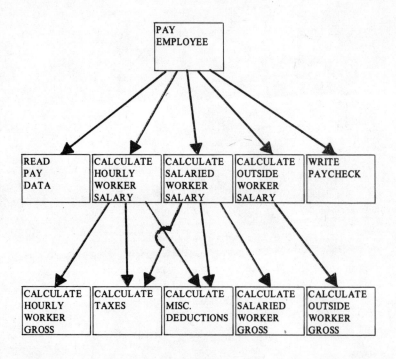

Which design is better — the one above, or the one discussed in Section 8.2? Perhaps our first design was better; after all, it had fewer boxes. Or, perhaps the design shown above is better; after all, it has boxes that individually carry out smaller (and presumably simpler) tasks. Obviously, we need some method of determining which of these hierarchies is "better" — that is, better in the sense discussed in Section 8.1. Which of the designs is more likely to be correct? Which design is easier to understand? Which design will be easier to modify? Which design will be more economical to develop and operate?

One method of evaluating a structure chart is to investigate the relationship between instructions inside a module, as well as the relationship between the modules themselves. In order to understand the entire system, we should be able to focus our attention on one module at a time — without having to worry about its interaction with various other modules in the system. Thus, the fewer interactions between modules on the structure chart, the more likely it is that the design will be easy to understand and easy to modify.

Paradoxically, the easiest way to make certain that the modules in a system are not too highly interrelated is to ensure that the individual instructions inside each module are very highly interrelated. That is, the instructions inside any single module should all be involved in the same task — a *single* task.

This concept of relatedness among instructions inside a module (or, more generally, the strength of association of subordinates to a given module) is known as *cohesion*. The more highly cohesive a module is, the more likely that module is involved in a single, well-defined task — and, as a corollary, the less likely that module will have subtle, unclear connections with other modules in the system.

The best — or strongest — type of cohesion that a module can display is *functional* cohesion: All of the instructions in the module work together to carry out one, and only one, task. For example, CALCULATE HOURLY WORKER GROSS is a functionally cohesive module. It does not calculate gross salary for all types of workers. It does not do anything special with some hourly workers; it does nothing but calculate the gross salary for hourly workers, using the same algorithm each time it is activated.

A module is considered *logically* cohesive when it carries out tasks that seem similar, but are not related in any way pertinent to the problem being solved. For example, we would consider CALCULATE TAXES to be a logically cohesive module, because it does many similar tasks: It calculates federal, state, local, and FICA taxes. Some employees may not have to pay local taxes; others may have already paid their full share of FICA taxes and need no further deduction in that category for the rest of the year.

As a result, we would expect CALCULATE-TAXES to be fairly large and complicated, particularly since it is common for programmers to take advantage of apparently similar logic situations in the processing of federal, state, local, and FICA taxes. The result could well be a module for which a modification to the federal tax logic would cause unexpected bugs in the FICA tax calculations.

In general, we try to avoid logically cohesive modules. While we cannot guarantee that such modules will be difficult to understand or modify, it seems silly to gamble. Virtually no extra work is required (and it is, indeed, often more efficient) to break a logically cohesive module into separate, functionally cohesive modules.

When we are designing a COBOL program, we should not worry too much about the eventual size of the various modules; instead, we should concern ourselves with the function of the modules. If it turns out that a functionally cohesive module is "trivial" (i.e., contains only a few COBOL statements), we may decide to incorporate it internally within the next higher-level superordinate. This decision should be made only after we have finished the design, and have convinced ourselves that the design is satisfactory. The decision to "push" a module into its superordinate is shown on a structure chart in the following way:

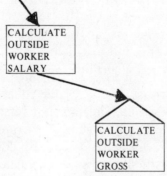

In the illustration, the triangular "hat" on CALCULATE OUTSIDE WORKER GROSS means that it is "lexically included" in the higher-level module that invokes it. When we read the code for this program, we will find the code to calculate an outside worker's gross salary within the module CALCULATE OUTSIDE WORKER SALARY.

Another thing we can look for in a design is so-called black-box behavior. A black box is any construct that can be used without any knowledge of its internal workings. We can make use of a black box if we know what inputs it requires, what outputs it will produce, and what its function is.

A good example of a black box, for most of us, is the common automobile. We know its inputs: gasoline, oil, water, and an occasional kick when it doesn't start. We know its outputs: energy used to spin the rear wheels. And we know its function: to transport a moderate number of people over a moderate distance for a moderate amount of money, within certain safety constraints. Most of us cannot explain the workings of a combustion engine, how the automobile is put together on an assembly line, or even how the cigarette lighter works. Fortunately, most states in the U.S. do not require such knowledge in order to obtain a driver's license!

Following is an example of a black-box module: You are writing a program that issues assignments to secret agents. The boss does not want any one programmer to know everything about the system. You must write the part of the program that matches assignments with free, qualified agents. Once an agent is eligible and meets the requirements, you must check a top-secret subroutine for the final approval. This subroutine is so secret, in fact, that the boss does not want you to know *anything* about how it works. You are given your instructions:

When you are ready to make the final check before assigning an agent, code PERFORM SECRET-OK CHECK. Make sure that you have defined the agent's code number as AGENT-CODE-NO, and the assignment code as MISSION-CODE.

Also, define a four-position alphanumeric switch called SECRET-OK. After PERFORMing this subroutine, the SECRET-OK indicator will be set to "OKAY" if the agent is cleared, or "NYET" if the agent cannot be assigned to this mission.

Your structure chart might look as follows:

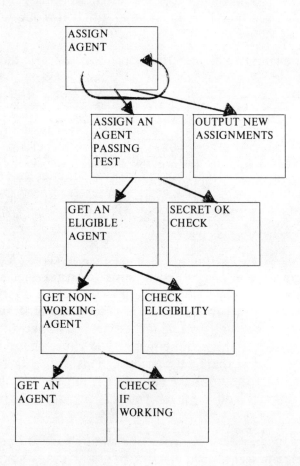

ASSIGN AN AGENT PASSING TEST, the module which invokes the secret subroutine, knows that the subroutine checks eligibility, but does not know how. It does not even know whether SECRET-OK CHECK is one module, or only the topmost of many modules. The important thing to remember is, it doesn't *need* to know.

When we use black-box modules, each module knows only of the existence of those modules that it invokes. This is of great benefit to programmers. For example, what if the rules for SECRET-OK CHECK need to be changed? Someone can change that module without affecting the other modules.

We do not have to work for a spy ring to realize that black-box modules make future modifications easier. By using black boxes wherever we can, we limit the impact of many changes.

Another way of evaluating a structure chart is to examine the nature and strength of the interactions between one module and another. We use the term *coupling* to describe the strength of connections between one module and another. As you would expect, our goal is to develop systems with loosely coupled modules, so that a modification of one module will have a minimum chance of affecting some other module. For example, the SECRET-OK CHECK module is loosely coupled to the other modules in the system, because it needs only a small amount of information — AGENT-CODE-NO, MISSION-CODE, and SECRET-OK — to do its work.

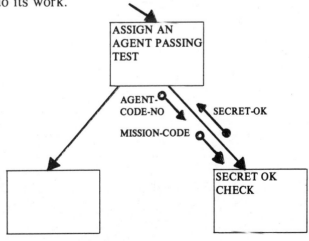

One method of evaluating the coupling between modules is to check the number of data items they must share. The fewer the items of data shared between modules, the more loosely coupled the design. If we pass many switches, indicators, and data items between modules, it becomes more likely that a modification to one module will affect some other module.

Coupling often can be reduced by rearranging the existing hierarchy of modules. As an example, consider the following extension to the spy design described above. Our spy ring uses its computer to write out "The Secret Code Word for the Day" to its agents. Because the word is top-secret, the keypunch operators punch only one letter per card. No single keypunch operator punches more than one letter; therefore, only the boss, who collates the cards, knows the entire word. The boss inserts dummy input before and after the code word, so that the computer operators will have little chance of determining the code word when they read the cards into the program. The word begins immediately after a card with a zero in column 1, and ends with a card containing a zero in column 1. In the example below, the code word is SNEAKY.

Below are two designs, labeled "Version 1" and "Version 2." From our description of the problem, you should be able to determine the interfaces between the modules — i.e., the data and control information that must pass between the various modules. When you do this, you should be able to decide which is better.

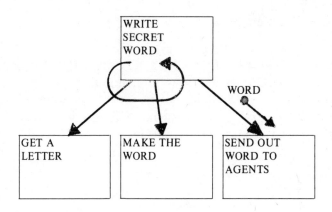

Version 1

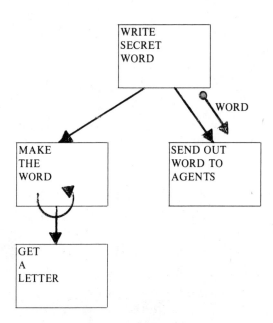

Version 2

The modules in Version 2 are less strongly coupled; therefore, we would judge that to be the better design. By contrast, note that in Version 1, MAKE THE WORD must return a flag to WRITE SECRET WORD to indicate whether it has finished making a word. Note that Version 2 does not require any flags.

In most cases, strong coupling between modules is an indication of low cohesion; conversely, a system with highly cohesive modules usually exhibits very low intermodular coupling. As an example, consider the following structure chart with a logically cohesive module FORMAT ALL ERRORS. (By the way, can you tell why it is a logically cohesive module?)

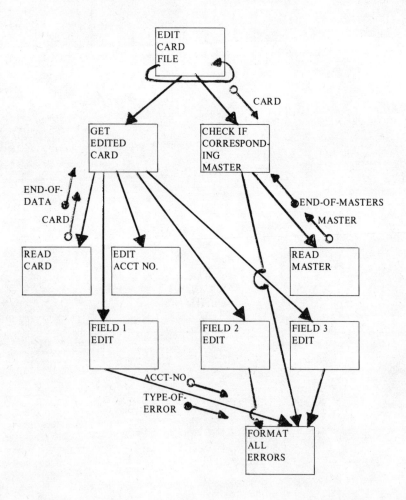

The program shown above edits cards that have an account number and three fields of information on them. The cards will be used by another program to update certain fields of a master file once they have been accepted by this editing program. Notice that the logically cohesive module requires a flag to determine *which* error has occurred. Now compare that structure chart with the following one:

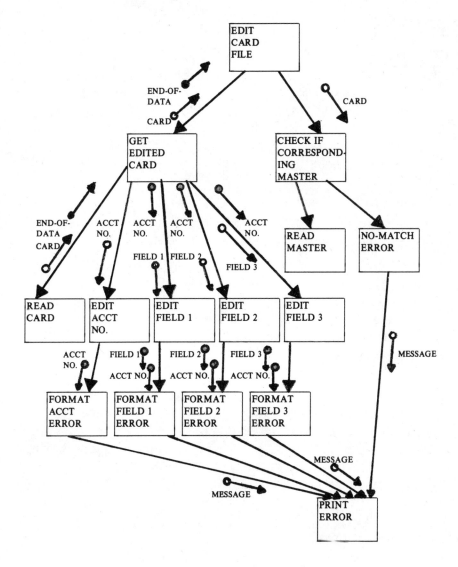

In this second design, the functionally cohesive error modules require no flag at all. If, during the actual coding of these modules, we discover that they are too small (i.e., only a few COBOL statements), then we can always "push them up" into their superordinate.

8.4 COBOL modules and connections

Thus far, we have concentrated on program design without much regard for COBOL. This has been intentional. Our concepts of good design practice are independent of any specific programming language. That is, we should strive for highly cohesive, loosely coupled, black-box modules regardless of the programming language we use — and it *is* possible to develop such modules, regardless of whether we code in FORTRAN, COBOL, or PL/I.

Nevertheless, our interest in this book obviously is in the development of COBOL modules; so let's turn our attention to the design of good programs and good modules in COBOL.

We'll begin with a careful definition of a module. In formal terms, a program module is usually defined as a contiguous group of statements having a single name by which it can be invoked as a unit.[3] In COBOL, this means that a module — i.e., one of the rectangular boxes drawn in a structure chart — can be either a paragraph, a SECTION, or an entire COBOL program.

We have not yet looked at an example of a SECTION in the PROCEDURE DIVISION; the code that follows illustrates this portion of a module. As you will see in the example, the SECTION is one method of grouping statements under a single name. A SECTION consists of zero or more paragraphs, each paragraph having its own COBOL statements. The SECTION must be given a name, immediately followed by the key word SECTION and a

---

[3]For a precise definition of module, see *Structured Design* by Edward Yourdon and Larry L. Constantine (New York: YOURDON inc., 1975).

period. A SECTION ends when another SECTION begins, or when the PROCEDURE DIVISION ends.

```
          EDIT-FIELDS SECTION.
          EDIT-ACCT-NO.
              ----------.
              ----------.
              ----------.
          EDIT-ZIP-CODE.
              ----------.
              ----------.
              ----------.
          EDIT-PHONE-NO.
              ----------.
              ----------.
              ----------.
          UPDATING SECTION.
```

The PERFORM statement is used to transfer control from one module to another, regardless of whether the module consists of a paragraph or a SECTION. Thus, we might find ourselves connecting paragraphs by coding:

```
          FILL-ORDER.
              ----------.
              ----------.
              ----------.
          PERFORM EDIT-PHONE-NO.
```

Equivalently, we might connect sections this way:

```
          FILL-ORDER SECTION.
              ----------.
              ----------.
              ----------.
          PERFORM EDIT-FIELDS.
```

We prefer to use paragraphs as the building block for modules. Our primary reason for this preference is that the use of paragraphs ensures that there will be only one way of entering the module (via the paragraph-name), and only one way of leaving the module (by returning to the module which PERFORMed the paragraph). Thus, we find that COBOL programs built from paragraphs tend to have the black-box behavior that we discussed in Section 8.3.

We are less able to guarantee this black-box behavior when we use SECTIONs as the basic building block of a COBOL program. To illustrate the problem, recall the example of the EDIT-FIELDS SECTION code above. It is possible that some other module in the program may contain the statement

PERFORM EDIT-ZIP-CODE.

Although this is perfectly legal, it is poor COBOL practice. Why? Because the module which contains this PERFORM statement obviously knows that the EDIT-FIELDS SECTION module has a side-door entrance named EDIT-ZIP-CODE. The black-box quality of EDIT-FIELDS is now seriously impaired. In general, a SECTION may have many such possible entry points (the SECTION name, plus all of the paragraph-names within it); it is therefore more difficult to maintain as a black box.

You may find that your programming group uses SECTIONs instead of paragraphs; indeed, there are some situations in which SECTIONs are highly desirable (e.g., to simulate a CASE structure), or absolutely necessary (e.g., in conjunction with the SORT verb, discussed in Chapter 13). From our discussion, you can see that the best approach is one of consistency: To form modules, you should either use SECTIONs consistently, or you should use paragraphs consistently. And, if you do use SECTIONs, be sure to avoid any temptation to PERFORM individual paragraphs within a SECTION.

Unfortunately, there is some confusion when we use paragraphs as the basic form of a module. Because of some quirks in the COBOL language, not every paragraph is a "meaningful" module. For example, consider the following program which copies card images onto magnetic tape:

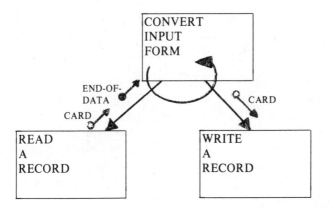

The structure chart is fairly straightforward; we can see that there are three modules. Now, let's look at the code:

```
PROCEDURE DIVISION.
A1-CONVERT-INPUT-FORM.
    OPEN RECD-IN INPUT
        RECD-OUT OUTPUT.
    MOVE 'NO' TO RECD-EOF.
    PERFORM B1-READ-A-RECORD.
    PERFORM PROCESS-LOOP
        UNTIL RECD-EOF = 'YES'.
    CLOSE RECD-IN
        RECD-OUT.
    STOP RUN.
PROCESS-LOOP.
    MOVE INPUT-RECORD TO OUTPUT-RECORD.
    PERFORM B2-WRITE-A-RECORD.
    PERFORM B1-READ-A-RECORD.
B1-READ-A-RECORD.
    READ RECD-IN
        AT END
            MOVE 'YES' TO RECD-EOF.
B2-WRITE-A-RECORD.
    WRITE OUTPUT-RECORD.
```

Note that PROCESS-LOOP exists because we need a paragraph-name for the PERFORM-UNTIL statement — that is, PROCESS-LOOP contains all those statements which may be executed iteratively. It did not appear in the structure chart because it never occurred to the designer to identify it as a distinct module; PROCESS-LOOP is only the body of a loop, and is really only a fragment of a "meaningful" module.

So what should we do about all of this? Most COBOL programmers prefer to think of a module like PROCESS-LOOP as an "artificial" module. They do not show it on their structure chart, but they do ensure that, in the program listing, PROCESS-LOOP is placed near the module containing the PERFORM-UNTIL which invokes PROCESS-LOOP. Other COBOL programmers feel that there should be a strict one-to-one correspondence between the paragraphs in their program and the rectangular boxes in their structure chart. Such programmers would deal with the situation by drawing the structure chart as follows:

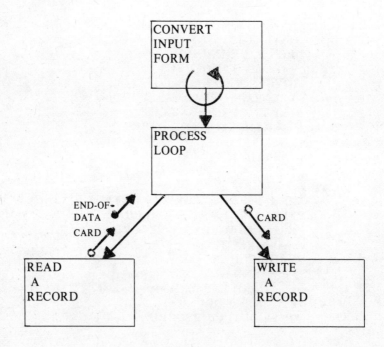

Once again, our primary concern is that you do things in a consistent fashion; most COBOL programmers will be able to understand either approach, as long as consistency is maintained.

Q. In the example above, how many times will PROCESS-LOOP be PERFORMed?

A. Once for each record in the RECD-IN file. The loop exits when RECD-EOF = 'YES', and 'YES' is moved to that flag when the RECD-IN file is AT END. Don't forget that the imperative clause following AT END is executed the *first* time there are no more records. If we try to READ after we have executed the AT END clause, the program will almost certainly abort (or it will begin to behave in an undefined fashion).

Q. Is the previous answer true under all possible conditions?

A. Yes, it is. If the file has no records, then the PROCESS-LOOP will never be executed. This is because the PERFORM-UNTIL statement tests its termination clause *before* executing the specified paragraph.

8.5 Program-to-program linkage

In the previous section, we mentioned some of the advantages and disadvantages of paragraphs and SECTIONs. There is an additional disadvantage of both paragraphs and SECTIONs that we should mention: By definition, any paragraph and any SECTION may access any data elements defined in the DATA DIVISION, regardless of whether the module has any legitimate reason for accessing the data.

For example, one module may require a field of data, properly defined in the DATA DIVISION, to hold an intermediate value when carrying out its calculations. No other module needs to know that this field even exists, yet every module in the program has the ability to refer to this field or even alter it. As you can imagine, this has serious consequences for maintenance and debugging.

Think, for example, of a large COBOL program (by large, we mean any program larger than 10,000 COBOL statements — many programs in industry today are more than 100,000 statements long!), which you have to modify. If you need to alter the length of a field, then you must find every reference to that field in the entire program; this is crucial, for you must ensure that the unchanged code (code in modules other than the ones you explicitly intended to modify) still will work correctly when the data field is changed. If your compiler does not produce a cross-reference listing of all data elements, this job will be tedious and error-prone — you may easily miss an obscure reference to your data element.

Q.   How is it possible that some code in other parts of a program may stop working correctly if the length of a field is changed?

A.   It is possible because the code may have made assumptions about the size of a number that the field contained. If the code assumes that the field never contains a number larger than 99 (decimal), peculiar things then would happen if the field were changed to a PIC 9(3).

The point of all this is very simple: If we partition code in the PROCEDURE DIVISION into black-box modules, then we should also try to partition data in the DATA DIVISION so that modules can access only that data which they require in order to carry out their function. How can we do this?

The most straightforward way, in COBOL, is to make each module a separately compiled program, rather than a paragraph or a SECTION. It is not necessary for a COBOL program to be invoked directly by the operating system on our computer; indeed, it is relatively easy to write programs that are invoked by other COBOL programs!

Remember the SECRET OK CHECK module that some other programmer wrote? Well, it turns out that the boss has decided to make that subroutine a separate program — and he wants you to fix your code to accommodate this change. (In case you have forgotten, you wrote the rest of the modules shown on the structure chart.) The name for the new program is SECRETOK.

Somewhere in ASSIGN AN AGENT PASSING TEST, you might find the statement

PERFORM SECRET-OK-CHECK.

If you changed that statement to

PERFORM SECRETOK.

the COBOL compiler would flag it. Why? Because it is illegal to PERFORM an entire COBOL program. If you compiled the program with the PERFORM statement shown above, the compiler would certainly produce an error message — for the simple reason that it could not find a paragraph named SECRETOK in your program.

So how does it work? We need a new statement that will allow one COBOL program to pass control to another. That statement is known as the CALL statement, discussed below.

8.6 The CALL statement

To connect one COBOL program to another, you must use the CALL statement. For example, in our spy system, we would simply change the PERFORM statement to read

CALL SECRETOK.

The CALL statement functions just like the PERFORM statement, except that it is used to connect two programs: the one containing the CALL, and the one named in the CALL statement.

Q.   If you saw the program SECRETOK, where do you think that name would be defined?

A.   In the PROGRAM-ID. You would find the statement

PROGRAM-ID. SECRETOK.

As you may remember, the SECRET OK CHECK module (when it was in the form of a paragraph) required the agent code and the mission code as its input; it returned the authorization status flag as its output. SECRETOK, the COBOL program, still needs the input codes, and must still produce the flag as its output. Somehow, we must be able to pass the necessary information between two programs. (Remember, each program has its own FILE SECTION and WORKING-STORAGE SECTION.) With the COBOL mechanisms that we have discussed up to this point, it is not possible to refer to fields defined outside the boundaries of a program.

In order to pass information across program boundaries, the CALLing program must explicitly state to what data the receiving program may refer. This is done with the USING option of the CALL statement. Since we must pass the two fields and the flag, the CALL statement will look like this:

CALL SECRETOK
**   USING   MISSION-CODE**
**   AGENT-CODE-NO**
**   SECRET-OKAY.**

The rules of the CALL-USING statement are: Every data-name in the USING clause must be defined with an 01- or 77-level-number in the CALLing program. The data-names may be defined in the FILE SECTION or the WORKING-STORAGE SECTION.

Incidentally, although the CALL acts somewhat like the PER-FORM statement, it does not have precisely the same syntax. For example, it is illegal to write

```
CALL SUB-PGM
    USING AFIELD
    UNTIL X = Y.
```

Unfortunately, the CALL statement may have only the USING option; however, the USING option is not necessary if the CALLing program does not need to pass any information to the CALLed program.

Q.   How would you accomplish the kind of logic that was attempted with the illegal CALL statement shown above? That is, how can you call a sub-program iteratively?

A.   The following code is the most common approach used by COBOL programmers:

```
PERFORM SUB-PGM-LOOP UNTIL X = Y.
    ----------.
    ----------.
    ----------.
SUB-PGM-LOOP.
    CALL SUB-PGM
        USING AFIELD.
```

8.7 The LINKAGE SECTION

Now that we've introduced the CALL statement, let's look at the new version of SECRETOK. If we were to look at its listing, we would immediately notice a new SECTION — something called the LINKAGE SECTION. The LINKAGE SECTION is the receiving end of the data passed in the CALL statement, and it is coded immediately after the WORKING-STORAGE SECTION. The LINKAGE SECTION for SECRETOK appears on the following page.

```
LINKAGE SECTION.
01   CODE-FOR-MISSION          PIC 9(5).
01   AGENT-ID-CODE             PIC 9(4).
01   CLEARANCE-FLAG            PIC X(3).

PROCEDURE DIVISION
     USING     CODE-FOR-MISSION
               AGENT-ID-CODE
               CLEARANCE-FLAG.
```

It may appear to you that there is a mistake here. After all, the CALLing statement was

```
CALL SECRETOK
     USING     MISSION-CODE
               AGENT-CODE-NO
               SECRET-OKAY.
```

All of this is perfectly legal. The data-names in the LINKAGE SECTION of the CALLed program need not be the same as the data-names in the CALLing program; indeed, if the two programs were written by different people at different times, it is unlikely that they would be identical. However, the data-names in the CALLed program and the CALLing program must describe data that are of the same length (and preferably of the same type) because the CALLed program will actually access the data in the CALLing program's DATA DIVISION. It is also important that the two programs agree on the order (or sequence) of the data elements. The order of the data elements is established by the US-ING clause in the PROCEDURE DIVISION statement of the CALLed program. Thus, we have the following correspondence in the SECRETOK situation:

	1st	2nd	3rd
CALL SECRETOK			
USING	MISSION-CODE	AGENT-CODE-NO	SECRET-OKAY.
PROCEDURE DIVISION			
USING	CODE-FOR-MISSION	AGENT-ID-CODE	CLEARANCE-FLAG.

Every field passed in a CALL must be defined in the LINK-AGE SECTION as an 01-level or 77-level entry. However, you are free to subdivide the fields in any way you find convenient — just as you would with data elements defined in the FILE SECTION or the WORKING-STORAGE SECTION. Thus, we might find that SECRETOK's LINKAGE SECTION would look like this:

```
LINKAGE SECTION.
01   CODE-FOR-MISSION.
     05   AREA-CODE                      PIC 9(2).
     05   DANGER-LEVEL                   PIC 9.
     05   SECRECY-LEVEL                  PIC 9(2).
01   AGENT-ID-CODE.
     05   AGENT-NUM                      PIC 9(2).
     05   AGENT-SECURITY-CLEARANCE       PIC 9.
     05   AGENT-PROFICIENCY-RATING       PIC 9.
01   CLEARANCE-FLAG                      PIC X(3).
PROCEDURE DIVISION
         USING     CODE-FOR-MISSION
                   AGENT-ID-CODE
                   CLEARANCE FLAG.
```

When the CALL statement is executed, control is passed to the SECRETOK program. Execution begins with the first statement in the PROCEDURE DIVISION of SECRETOK, as you would expect. SECRETOK carries out its prescribed task of deciding whether the specified agent qualifies for the assignment, and then returns to the program that CALLed it.

How does SECRETOK know where to return, and how does it actually accomplish this return? Unlike paragraphs and SECTIONs (which exit when the end of the PROCEDURE DIVISION is reached, or when another paragraph or SECTION is encountered), and unlike programs invoked directly by the operating system (which exit to the operating system when a STOP RUN statement is encountered), a CALLed subprogram must explicitly exit by executing an EXIT PROGRAM statement. This statement has a simple syntax: It must be the only statement in a sentence; that sentence must be the only one in the paragraph. Thus, SECRETOK probably would contain a paragraph like this:

```
SECRETOK-EXIT.
    EXIT PROGRAM.
```

Here is a graphic representation of the communication between CALLing and CALLed COBOL programs:

CALLING PROGRAM.   SECRETOK PROGRAM.

```
----------.                         PROGRAM-ID. SECRETOK.
----------.                         LINKAGE SECTION.
----------.                         01    CODE-FOR-MISSION  PIC 9(5).
----------.                         01    AGENT-CODE        PIC 9(4).
----------.                         01    CLEARANCE-FLAG    PIC X(3).
CALL SECRETOK                       PROCEDURE DIVISION
   USING                               USING
      MISSION-CODE                        CODE-FOR-MISSION
      AGENT-NO                            AGENT-CODE
      SECRET-OKAY.                        CLEARANCE-FLAG.
IF SECRET-OKAY = 'YES'                 ----------.
   ----------                          ----------.
   ----------                          ----------.
ELSE                                   ----------.
   ----------                          ----------.
   ----------.                      EXIT-SECRETOK.
----------.                            EXIT PROGRAM.
```

8.8 Using CALL to build systems

In developing large systems, veteran COBOL programmers use CALLed programs as their basic building block. This approach enables them to modify and recompile one program without necessarily having to modify or recompile any other programs in the system. In addition, the use of the LINKAGE SECTION forces the designer to define, explicitly, the interfaces between the modules. By contrast, designers who use paragraphs or SECTIONs as their basic building block often find that they have ignored the intermodular interfaces.

To illustrate the use of CALLed modules in a COBOL system, let's consider the design of an editing system for an airline charter business having the unlikely name of Wing-and-a-Prayer Charter Tours. It happens that business has increased so much at W&P that the company is beginning to computerize its current manual charter air tour system, which is known as CATS.

Our task is to design a program that will edit the incoming client transactions. These transactions eventually will be used to update the charter tour master file so that clients can be booked on their choice of tours.

The input to the program is shown in Table 8.1 on the following page. Each client has one record, occupying an 80-position card. There will be two outputs from the program: an Edited Client File (ready for further processing), and a listing of the errors that were found. Each input record either will generate an output record on the Edited Client File, or will generate a message on the error listing. The format of the Edited Client File is identical to that of the card input file. The general format of the error listing is shown in Table 8.2. The precise format of the error messages is up to you; just be sure that they are appropriate.

The input cards have already been organized in ascending order by Tour Number; within every tour, clients are batched together by group. A group is identified by client records with the same Client Number. The Number in Group field should contain the same number as there are clients with identical Client Numbers. If there is disagreement, an error should be noted.

As you can see in Table 8.1, the editing criteria are fairly straightforward. However, a few of the edits merit special explanation. The Airport Choice code is the three-letter international airport code; it should be a three-character alphabetic field. For example, LAX is the official designation for the Los Angeles International Airport. Unfortunately, W&P only operates from a few airports; here is a list of the acceptable airports:

JFK	John F. Kennedy Airport, New York
ORD	O'Hare Airport, Chicago
LAX	Los Angeles International Airport
SFO	San Francisco International Airport
DFW	Dallas/Fort Worth Airport
IAD	Dulles Airport, Washington, D.C.

Any airport code other than the ones listed above should be treated as an error.

Table 8.1. Format of input cards.

FIELD NAME	LENGTH	EDITING CRITERIA	POSITIONS
Tour Number	4 positions	numeric	pos 1-4
Client Number	4 positions	numeric	pos 5-8
Number in Group	1 position	numeric	pos 9
1st Airport Choice	3 positions	alpha	pos 10-12
1st Airline Choice	2 positions	alpha	pos 13-14
1st Flight Number	3 positions	numeric	pos 15-17
1st Seating Choice	1 position	numeric	pos 18
*2nd Airport Choice	3 positions	alpha or blank	pos 19-21
*2nd Airline Choice	2 positions	alpha or blank	pos 22-23
*2nd Flight Number	3 positions	numeric or blank	pos 24-26
*2nd Seating Choice	1 position	numeric or blank	pos 27
Client Name	15 positions	must be present	pos 28-42
Street Address	16 positions	must be present	pos 43-58
City	15 positions	must be present	pos 59-73
State	2 positions	alpha	pos 74-75
Zip Code	5 positions	numeric	pos 76-80

*For second-choice information to be valid, all fields must pass the specific edit or all must be blank.

Table 8.2. Layout of error listing.

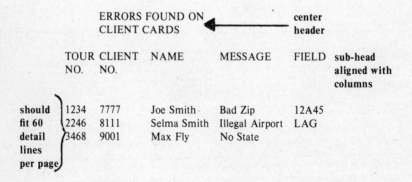

Airline Choice is the two-letter code for the airlines. W&P buys blocks of seats on regularly scheduled airlines for its charter tours. Depending on the airport, it uses certain carriers:

AIRPORT	CARRIERS			
JFK	TW	PA	BA	AF
ORD	PA	AM		
LAX	PA	QF	JA	
SFO	JA	PA	TW	
DFW	PA			
IAD	BW	AF	PA	AL

The airline abbreviations have the following meanings:

CODE	AIRLINE
TW	Trans World Airlines
PA	Pan American
BA	British Airways
AF	Air France
AM	Aeronaves de Mexico
JA	Japan Airlines
BW	British West Indies Airlines
AL	Alitalia Airlines
QF	Qantas Airways

Our program should permit only tours flying on authorized airlines (listed above) from authorized airports.

At the present time, W&P only requires a numeric editing test for the Flight Number field; at some later time, they may wish the test to be more sophisticated. The Seating Choice field should be either a 1 (for first class), or a 2 (for coach); any other code is an error.

If all of the individual Client Records pass the edits, then check to ensure that they all have the identical first-choice and second-choice airport/airline/flight/seating information. If they are truly a group, they must be traveling together!

If a group of records passes this final test, then each of the records in the group should be written to the Edited Client File. We are to write only those records which pass every edit, including the group edits.

Once you are certain that you understand the problem, develop a structure chart for your solution. Be sure that you show all of the data and control information that must be passed between the modules. Don't worry about the size of the modules now — your primary concern is to design modules of high cohesion and loose coupling. Take your time; nobody produces a good structure chart quickly for a problem of this size.

When you have finished your structure chart, look at the suggested solution in the Appendix. If yours differs dramatically, spend some time comparing the two. If you have any questions, this is a good time to talk to your instructor.

8.9 Structured program design methodologies

How did you arrive at the solution for the Wing-and-a-Prayer system in the previous section? Chances are, you used intuition to develop your solution — and you should be neither surprised nor disappointed if you had to scrap several poor designs before arriving at a good one. Nor should you be terribly disappointed if your design looks somewhat different from the one in this book.

Our solution for the W&P system — and most other systems discussed in this book — was developed with a methodology known as *transform analysis,* or *transform-centered design.* Transform-centered design is a "cookbook" approach that usually produces good designs (good from the point of view of cohesion and coupling) for common data processing applications. We shall provide only a brief summary of the design strategy here; for a more comprehensive discussion, consult Yourdon and Constantine's *Structured Design.* [4]

---

[4] Edward Yourdon and Larry L. Constantine, *Structured Design* (New York: YOURDON inc., 1975).

The first step in transform-centered design is to represent the problem in a nonprocedural form known as a program graph or bubble chart. You may recall seeing program graphs in the brief discussion of program design in Section 3.10 of Part 1 of this series. For the W&P system, the program graph can be drawn as follows:

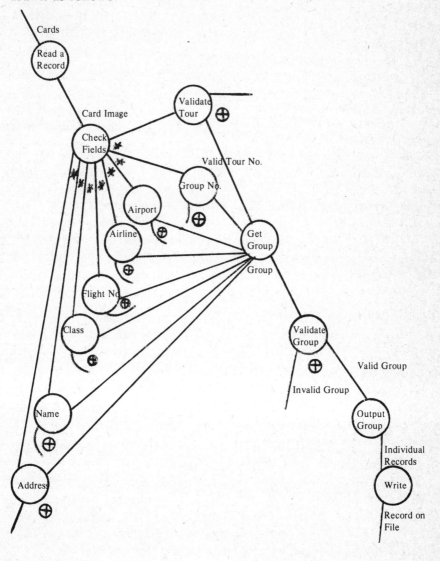

The second step is often described as "looking for the point of highest abstraction." We follow the flow of data along the program graph to see where the input ends — that is, the point where the data can no longer be regarded as input. In the case of the W&P system, card images are obviously input — indeed, the difference between a card image and a card is hardly more than semantic. The next recognizable piece of data in the program graph is the tour data associated with a "valid individual"; certainly, this type of data can still be regarded as input to the system.

The next type of data is a group of individuals; this is a more aggregate, and therefore more logical, form of data. Note, for example, that it is no longer evident at this stage whether the data has anything to do with such physical forms of data as a card image.

Finally, we see a valid group as the next form of data in the program graph. At this point, we know that each individual's tour has been checked, and that the individuals have been checked against one another for consistency. If we go one step further in the program graph, we find that we are dealing with an edited file record, which clearly represents an output from the W&P system. So, we determine that the most logical, or most highly processed, input to the W&P system is a valid group.

The third step of the transform-centered design strategy is to work our way backward from the output end(s) of the program graph, looking for the first point at which we have something resembling output. This, too, could be regarded as a point of highest abstraction — i.e., a form of data that is definitely an output from the system, but which has not yet been put into proper form for physical outputting.

In the case of the W&P system, we first notice a form of data that consists of a record to be written on an Edited Customer File. While this is definitely an output from the system, it is not necessarily the most logical output. Indeed, if we go inward (toward the middle of the program graph) one step further, we next find a valid group — a *collection* of records to be written. Recall that this was also the data element that we regarded as the most logical form of input — so there is no point tracing inward any further on the program graph for logical forms of output.

What does all this mean? Simply that the W&P system, at the highest level, appears to be a simple input-output program: It obtains valid groups of customers, then writes them to the Edited Customer File. Everything else in the program is a *detail* having to do with input or output. If we mark on the program graph where the input ends and the output begins, we would have something like this:

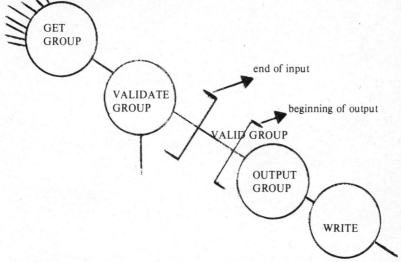

We must emphasize that the W&P system is unusually simple in that it has no calculations, or central transforms. Most of the COBOL programs that you develop will have a number of bubbles in the program graph *between* the point where input ends and the point where output begins.

After we have gotten this far, we can begin to build a structure chart. The purpose of finding the most logical inputs and the most logical outputs is to determine where the top-level module in the W&P system will be attached to other modules in the hierarchy. To see how this works, imagine the program graph as a collection of cardboard disks with pieces of string connecting them. Taking a pair of scissors, we snip the string at the end of the input, and again at the beginning of the output. Now we introduce a cardboard rectangle, which is named EDIT-CLIENT-TRANSACTIONS. It, too, has strings dangling from it.

Taking strings from the rectangle, we tie one to the snipped end of the input and another to the beginning of the output. If we lift the whole mess by the rectangle, we'll get something that looks like this:

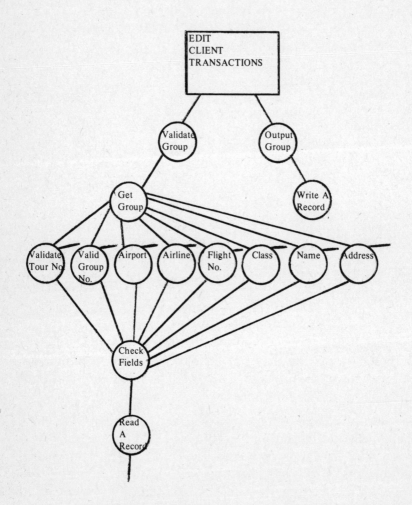

If we convert each bubble to a rectangular box, we can see that we have a rough approximation of a structure chart. Obviously, we need to further partition the modules into one or more levels of highly cohesive subordinate modules. And we must examine our structure chart for possible coupling problems, although they should be minimal if the program graph was drawn properly. Regardless of whether we implement the modules with CALLed subprograms of PERFORMed paragraphs (or SECTIONs), it is important that we give careful attention to the interfaces between the modules.

9 More Powerful Facilities

9.1 Traditional flowcharts

There's a good chance that your organization uses flowcharts as its documentation for each program. Flowcharts emphasize the procedural aspects of the program; they show every action and every decision, connected in the time-order in which they occur. For example, the flowchart on the following page shows a program that will read three cards and store them in three areas. If an end-of-file condition is noted, or if a blank card is found, the program finishes by setting the end-of-file indicator or blank-card indicator; if it finds three non-blank cards, it finishes without setting any indicator.

One alternative to the traditional flowchart is the so-called structured flowchart. Most people refer to it as a Nassi-Shneiderman diagram, named for Isaac Nassi and Ben Shneiderman, who first described the technique.[1] Compare the traditional flowchart on the next page with the Nassi-Shneiderman diagram of procedural logic that follows it. Both represent the same program that we saw before in flowchart form.

There is yet another alternative to the flowchart: *pseudocode,* also called structured English, program design language, or computer Esperanto. Its purpose is to give the programmer a good balance between the precision of programming languages like COBOL and the informality of English.

---

[1] I. Nassi and B. Shneiderman, "Flowchart Techniques for Structured Programming," *ACM SIGPLAN Notices,* Vol. 8, No. 8 (August 1973), pp. 12-26.

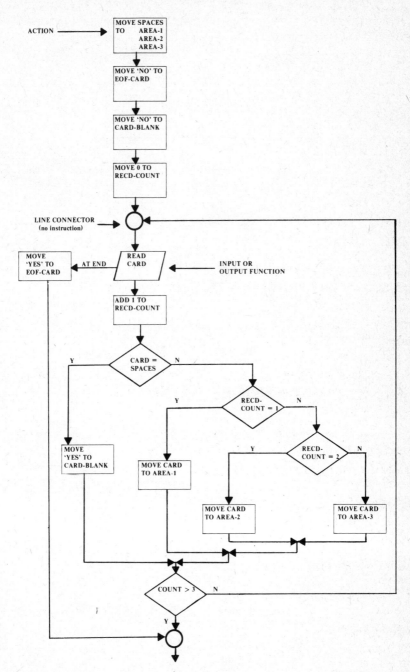

Traditional flowchart.

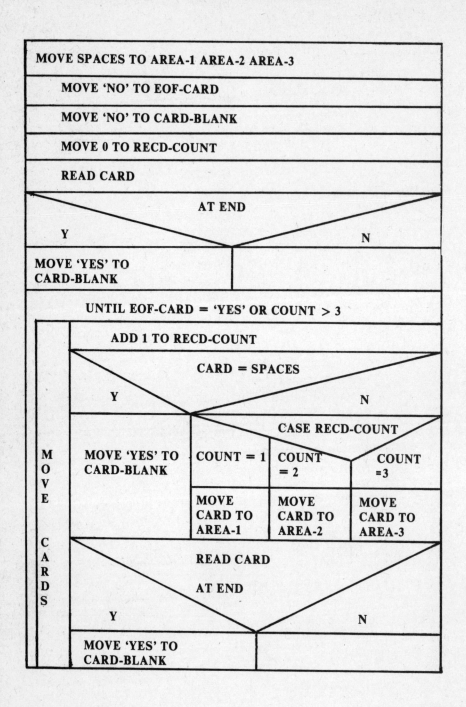

Nassi-Shneiderman diagram.

A pseudocode version of our simple card-reading program might look as follows:

```
MOVE SPACES TO AREA-1 AREA-2 AREA-3
MOVE 'NO' TO EOF-CARD
MOVE 'NO' TO CARD-BLANK
MOVE 0 TO RECD-COUNT
READ CARD
  AT END MOVE 'YES' TO EOF-CARD
UNTIL EOF-CARD = 'YES' OR RECD-COUNT > 3
  ADD 1 TO RECD-COUNT
  IF CARD = SPACES
     MOVE 'YES' TO CARD-BLANK
  ELSE IF RECD-COUNT = 1
     MOVE CARD TO AREA-1
  ELSE IF RECD-COUNT = 2
     MOVE CARD TO AREA-2
  ELSE
     MOVE CARD TO AREA-3.
```

Which form of procedural documentation should we use? The only proper answer is, use whatever works for you. Throughout the 1950's and 1960's, most EDP organizations used flowcharts; however, most programmers today agree that flowcharts have some major drawbacks. The first problem has to do with the correspondence between the flowchart and the COBOL code. You'll find that a strict interpretation of the flowchart almost inevitably leads to coding with GO TO statements, which we try to avoid.

A more significant problem has to do with maintenance. If we change the COBOL coding, what are the chances that the flowchart will be modified appropriately? Most EDP organizations have found that it is almost impossible to guarantee that the flowcharts and the COBOL coding will remain consistent after several years of maintenance. Indeed, it is very common to find that a programmer will not draw the flowchart for his program until *after* he has finished debugging the program! This means that he will have a flowchart of what he thinks his program is doing, which may or may not be the same as what his program really is doing.

This emphasizes an important point about detailed documentation for our programs. When a program is modified, what happens if the COBOL coding and the documentation disagree? Obviously, we are forced to believe the code, since that is what the computer executes. Thus, if there is any chance that the documentation will *not* be updated when the code is updated, the documentation is worthless. There are three ways of interpreting this observation:

1.   Maintaining the current documentation for a program is as important as maintaining the code itself.

2.   The form of documentation should be something that a programmer will find *easy* to maintain. If the documentation is difficult or awkward to update, there is more chance that it will be ignored. This would suggest that pseudocode is the best form of documentation, since it is the easiest for the programmer to generate. The problem with both Nassi-Shneiderman diagrams and flowcharts is that they require the programmer to become involved with "artwork"; chances are that it will be done sloppily if a maintenance effort has to be done in the middle of the night.

3.   In a real-world environment, there is a good chance that *no* detailed documentation will be kept up-to-date. We feel — based on our own experience — that the most reliable form of documentation is a standard structure chart (which does not change very much during maintenance), combined with neat, formatted, COBOL source code.

9.2 Details of the PERFORM statement

In addition to the MOVE statement and the arithmetic statements, the statement we will use most often is the PERFORM. Therefore, it is imperative that we thoroughly understand its capabilities.

Thus far, we have used the simple PERFORM as a connector of two modules:

PERFORM EDIT-ACCT-NUM.

However, there is another version of the PERFORM which can be used as a connector. It is the PERFORM-THRU, illustrated by the following statement:

PERFORM EDIT-ACCT-NUM THRU EDIT-ZIP-CODE.

This version of the PERFORM statement will pass control to the EDIT-ACCT-NUM paragraph; execution will then continue through *all* of the paragraphs following EDIT-ACCT-NUM until EDIT-ZIP-CODE is reached. EDIT-ZIP-CODE will be executed, too — and, at its conclusion, control will return to the statement immediately following the PERFORM THRU.

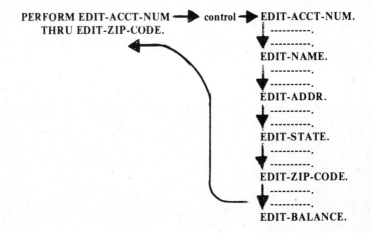

Although the PERFORM-THRU is legal in COBOL, we prefer to use the simple version of the PERFORM. Adapting the example shown above, we would write:

```
PERFORM EDIT-ACCT-NUM.
PERFORM EDIT-NAME.
PERFORM EDIT-ADDR.
PERFORM EDIT-STATE.
PERFORM EDIT-ZIP-CODE.
```

Why do we prefer the simple version of the PERFORM? It allows us to insert extra paragraphs among the existing EDIT paragraphs without affecting the nature of the control logic. With the PERFORM-THRU, the EDIT paragraphs are strongly coupled together; they *must* remain physically adjacent, and no new code may be inserted without affecting what happens when the PERFORM-THRU is executed. We've learned, after many long nights of debugging, that it's dangerous to depend upon the fact that control "falls" from one paragraph to the next.

Some programmers use the PERFORM-THRU as the standard connection between COBOL paragraphs. In such cases, the custom is to follow each paragraph with an EXIT paragraph. Thus, we might see code like this:

```
PERFORM EDIT-ACCT-NUM THRU EDIT-ACCT-EXIT.
----------------.
EDIT-ACCT-NUM.
    ----------.
    ----------.
    ----------.
EDIT-ACCT-EXIT.
    EXIT.
```

The EXIT statement must appear as the only statement in a paragraph; its sole purpose is to mark the *end* of a procedure — in this case, the account-number-edit procedure. Programmers often use this form of PERFORM-THRU in order to facilitate the use of GO TO statements *within* the procedure; e.g., to provide for an

early exit from the module by passing control to the EXIT paragraph. As an example, consider the following fragment of code:

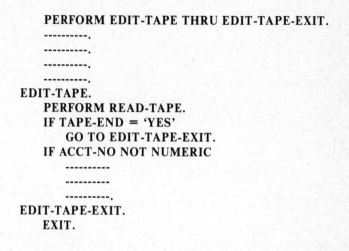

```
PERFORM EDIT-TAPE THRU EDIT-TAPE-EXIT.
----------.
----------.
----------.
----------.
EDIT-TAPE.
    PERFORM READ-TAPE.
    IF TAPE-END = 'YES'
        GO TO EDIT-TAPE-EXIT.
    IF ACCT-NO NOT NUMERIC
        ----------
        ----------
        ----------.
EDIT-TAPE-EXIT.
    EXIT.
```

The same logic could be coded without the GO TO statement as follows:

```
PERFORM EDIT-TAPE.
----------.
----------.
----------.
----------.
EDIT-TAPE.
    PERFORM READ-TAPE.
    IF TAPE-END = 'NO' AND
        ACCT-NO NOT NUMERIC
        ----------
        ----------
        ----------.
EDIT-TAPE-EXIT.
    EXIT.
```

Note that with this arrangement of code, the final EXIT paragraph
really isn't necessary. Indeed, this is generally true. If we organize our logic properly, the GO TO statement is superfluous.

Although we prefer the simple PERFORM as a connector between modules, you should follow whatever standards have been determined by your programming organization. The important thing, as always, is to be consistent.

9.3 The PERFORM-UNTIL statement

The PERFORM statement is used in yet another way: to form a *loop*. This is done with the PERFORM-UNTIL construct. An example of such a construct is

```
PERFORM PROCESS-RECDS
    UNTIL END-OF-RECDS = 'YES'.
```

The important thing about the PERFORM-UNTIL statement is that the UNTIL clause is tested *before* the specified paragraph is invoked. Thus, if END-OF-RECDS had been set to 'YES' *before* the PERFORM-UNTIL statement was invoked, PROCESS-RECDS would be invoked *zero* times. For most normal applications, we would expect PROCESS-RECDS to be invoked at least once, and we would expect that the code within PROCESS-RECDS would eventually set END-OF-RECDS to 'YES'. But it is important to remember that the PERFORM-UNTIL statement may execute the specified paragraph zero times, since it tests the terminating condition before it carries out the PERFORM.

Obviously, you must plan your logic so as to take this into account. In the example above, the programmer might ensure that PROCESS-RECDS is executed at least once by explicitly initializing the value of END-OF-RECDS. Thus, we might see

```
MOVE 'NO' TO END-OF-RECDS.
PERFORM PROCESS-RECDS
    UNTIL END-OF-RECDS = 'YES'.
```

It is permissible to specify *compound* conditions in the UN-TIL clause of a PERFORM-UNTIL. For example, we might write

PERFORM PROCESS-RECDS
    UNTIL END-OF-RECDS = 'YES'
    OR BAD-RECD = 'YES'.

If you do use compound conditions, it is considered good style to enclose any pairs of conditions in parentheses. Thus, we might see code like this:

PERFORM PROCESS-RECDS
    UNTIL BAD-MSTR = 'YES'
    OR (END-TRANS = 'YES' AND END-MSTR = 'YES').

If we write the code this way, anyone reading it will understand exactly what conditions will cause the loop to terminate.

Note that the PERFORM-UNTIL statements we have seen will continue looping — i.e., continue invoking a named paragraph — until some *logical condition* occurs. We don't know when we write the code whether the loop will be executed six, one hundred, or one million times. Since there often are programming situations in which we *want* to specify the *number* of times the loop will execute, COBOL provides a TIMES option on the PER-FORM statement. Thus, we can write

PERFORM EDIT-FIELDS
    6 TIMES.

or

PERFORM EDIT-FIELDS
    NUMBER-OF-FIELDS TIMES.

If we use the second version of the TIMES option, we must be certain that the "iteration variable" — in this case, NUMBER-OF-

FIELDS — is defined as a *numeric integer.* If its value is negative or zero, then the specified paragraph, EDIT-FIELDS, will not be executed at all.

There is another restriction of which you should be aware: It is illegal to change the value of the iteration variable during the execution of the PERFORM-UNTIL statement. In the example above, we may not change the value of NUMBER-OF-FIELDS from the first time we invoke EDIT-FIELDS until after we have finished executing the entire PERFORM-UNTIL statement. After the PERFORM-UNTIL has finished executing, the value of the iteration variable will be the same as when we first began executing it; the looping process will not affect the field in any way.

In practice, we seldom use the TIMES option on the PER-FORM statement. In most situations, the programmer is unable to specify the number of iterations of a loop with a constant, or even with a simple variable. It is more common to introduce one variable to indicate which iteration is currently being performed, and another variable to indicate how many iterations should be carried out for this particular execution of the PER-FORM loop. We often see COBOL coding of the following sort:

```
    MOVE ZERO TO FIELD-NUMBER.
    PERFORM EDIT-FIELDS
        UNTIL FIELD-NUMBER = MAX-NUMBER-OF-FIELDS.
```

Note that we accomplished this loop — which is definitely of an iterative nature — with the familiar PERFORM-UNTIL construct that we discussed earlier.

We should point out that there often is more than one reason for terminating a loop. One terminating condition, for example, might be based on an iteration count, while another terminating condition might be based on a logical condition. As a result, we often see COBOL coding such as is shown on the following page:

MOVE ZERO TO FIELD-NUMBER.
PERFORM EDIT-FIELDS
      UNTIL FIELD-NUMBER = MAX-NUMBER-OF-FIELDS
         OR EDITING-ERROR = 'YES'.

Regardless of the type of PERFORM loop you code, there is one important rule to keep in mind: You *must* state the conditions of looping correctly. Common mistakes in this area are:

1. The programmer instinctively assumes that his PERFORM loop will be executed at least once — and fails to construct his logic so that the loop will "do nothing gracefully"[2] when the UNTIL clause is satisfied the first time it is tested.

2. The loop does not execute correctly on the first iteration — e.g., the programmer forgets to initialize subscripts or other variables properly for the first iteration of the loop.

3. The programmer fails to prepare correctly for the next iteration of the loop. Typically, the next iteration will require that the next transaction be read, or that a subscript be incremented.

4. The programmer fails to terminate the loop correctly. It is common for a loop to iterate one time too many, or one time too few; it is in this area that you must be particularly careful to remember that the UNTIL clause is tested *before* the specified paragraph is PERFORMed. On rare occasions, a programmer constructs an infinite loop — a loop that never terminates — but such a bug is so obvious that it is quickly remedied.

---

[2]B.W. Kernighan and P.J. Plauger, *The Elements of Programming Style* (New York: McGraw-Hill, 1974), p. 88.

Consider the following fragment of code, which reads through a sequentially ordered transaction file until it finds a transaction with an account number matching the account number of a master record:

```
PERFORM READ-TRANS
    UNTIL TRANS-ACCT = MSTR-ACCT.
```

But what if there is a transaction with no corresponding master record? If the transaction file is in ascending sequence by account number, we could code

```
PERFORM READ-TRANS
    UNTIL TRANS-ACCOUNT NOT < MSTR-ACCT.
IF TRANS-ACCT > MSTR-ACCT
    PERFORM NO-MATCH-TRANS
ELSE
    PERFORM MATCH-PROCESSING.
```

What must we be able to assert immediately before the PER-FORM? That we indeed have a master account number available for comparison! We need to ask ourselves if the master file could be at end of file when we execute the loop.

Before we code a loop, we must be able to convince ourselves that we have the necessary elements for proper control of the loop. The conditions for terminating the loop must be stated so that no matter what happens during the iterations of the loop, we will eventually exit. We must also ensure that the code following the PERFORM-UNTIL loop will be able to execute properly regardless of the reason for terminating the loop. Remember: Anything that *can* happen *will* happen, sooner or later — and it invariably will be the least convenient thing that happens. So, plan your loops with great care.

9.4 CASE structures with GO TO DEPENDING ON

It is common for a field — i.e., a variable — to have more than two possible values. In such situations, different actions that are dependent on those values usually must be taken. This is accomplished with a construct known as a CASE. We saw a structured flowchart of a CASE construct in Section 9.1, a portion of which is extracted as follows:

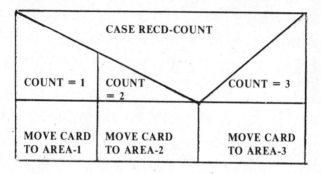

We could code this using IF-ELSE statements:

```
IF RECD-COUNT = 1
    MOVE CARD TO AREA-1
ELSE IF RECD-COUNT = 2
    MOVE CARD TO AREA-2
ELSE
    MOVE CARD TO AREA-3.
```

Note that we don't indent this code as we would with a nested IF statement. Why? Because the actions are mutually exclusive. In the code above, for instance, we move a card to only one area each time the code is activated. Since the actions are mutually exclusive, we arrange the indentation to emphasize that the actions occur at the same logical level. It is important to recognize that this indentation means nothing to the COBOL compiler, the operating system, or the computer hardware; it is done solely for the benefit of the human reader trying to understand what the author of the code intended.

There is another way to implement the CASE construct in COBOL, using the GO TO DEPENDING ON statement:

```
MOVE-CARD-TO-AREA.
     GO TO      RECD-AREA-1
                RECD-AREA-2
                RECD-AREA-3
                DEPENDING ON RECD-COUNT.
RECD-AREA-1.
   MOVE CARD TO AREA-1.
   GO TO AREA-EXIT.
RECD-AREA-2.
   MOVE CARD TO AREA-2.
   GO TO AREA-EXIT.
RECD-AREA-3.
   MOVE CARD TO AREA-3.
   GO TO AREA-EXIT.
AREA-EXIT.
   EXIT.
```

This piece of code could be executed using the statement

PERFORM MOVE-CARD-TO-AREA THRU AREA-EXIT.

Here, we have used a PERFORM-THRU to make it obvious to the reader of our program that the scope of the CASE construct is everything from the paragraph-name, MOVE-CARD-TO-AREA, to the final AREA-EXIT paragraph.

The rules of the GO TO DEPENDING ON statement are very restrictive. The field which is the object of the DEPENDING ON clause — RECD-COUNT in the example above — must contain a positive *numerical* value. Control is then transferred to the first, second, third, . . . or nth paragraph, depending on the numerical value of the field.

If the field contains a value that is "out of range," the GO TO DEPENDING ON is effectively ignored, and control is passed to the first statement *after* the GO TO DEPENDING ON. Looking back at our example, RECD-COUNT must contain the numerical value of 1, 2, or 3 in order for the code to behave in a meaningful way. If RECD-COUNT is zero, or 6, or 'YES', or *anything* but 1, 2, or 3, control will pass to the first statement after the GO TO DEPENDING ON — i.e., to paragraph RECD-AREA-1.

This can be a dangerous procedure: If there were a bug somewhere else in the program which caused RECD-COUNT to be set to some illegal value, the program could continue behaving as if everything were all right, and it might take quite a while to determine that RECD-COUNT was out of range.

Consequently, it is considered good programming style to introduce an error paragraph immediately following the GO TO DEPENDING ON statement — unless the object of the DEPENDING ON clause always can be guaranteed to be in range when the GO TO DEPENDING ON is encountered.

Q.   Does the following illustrate legal use of the GO TO DEPENDING ON statement?

```
REGION-CHECK.
      GO TO   EAST-REG
              EAST-REG
              CENTRAL-REG
              ROCKY-REG
              WEST-REG
              DEPENDING ON REGION-CODE.
ERROR-REG.
      ----------.
      ----------.
      GO TO REG-EXIT.
EAST-REG.
      ----------.
      ----------.
      GO TO REG-EXIT.
CENTRAL-REG.
      ----------.
      ----------.
      GO TO REG-EXIT.
ROCKY-REG.
      ----------.
      ----------.
      GO TO REG-EXIT.
WEST-REG.
      ----------.
      ----------.
      GO TO REG-EXIT.
REG-EXIT.
      EXIT.
```

A.   Yes, it is perfectly legal. Note that two values of REGION-CODE result in control being passed to the same paragraph.

Q.   What is the legal range of REGION-CODE in the example above?

A.   1 through 5, inclusive.

Q.   What would happen if there were no GO TO statements at the end of each paragraph, *and* the value of REGION-CODE were 1?

A.   Control would fall through all four paragraphs; that is, through EAST-REG, CENTRAL-REG, ROCKY-REG, and WEST-REG.

Q.   What would happen if the significant values of REGION-CODE were 1, 14, 60, and 94?

A.   We would have to list 94 paragraphs in the GO TO DEPENDING ON statement, all but four of which would cause control to be transferred to an error paragraph.

Q.   What would be a more straightforward way of coding the CASE construct if the values of REGION-CODE were 1, 14, 60, and 94?

A.   Using the IF-ELSE construct, we could build the following CASE mechanism:

```
IF REGION-CODE = 1
    ----------
    ----------
ELSE IF REGION-CODE = 14
    ----------
    ----------
ELSE IF REGION-CODE = 60
    ----------
    ----------
ELSE IF REGION-CODE = 94
    ----------
    ----------
ELSE
    PERFORM ERROR-ROUTINE.
```

(In the above example, the final ELSE clause is used to catch all situations in which REGION-CODE is not equal to 1, 14, 60, or 94.)

Unless circumstances *naturally* argue in favor of the GO TO DEPENDING ON construct, it is better style to use the IF-ELSE-IF construct for a CASE. We strongly recommend that you avoid converting a non-numeric field to a numeric value in order to take advantage of the GO TO DEPENDING ON. In most cases, the conversion is a waste of time — yours and the computer's. Similarly, we suggest that you avoid assigning clever, artificial numerical codes to variables, if your only reason for doing so is to take advantage of the GO TO DEPENDING ON. In such cases, the user of the program ends up having to remember the meaning of some arbitrary set of numerical codes, rather than having the convenience of mnemonic alphanumeric names for his data.

9.5 Literals, and why you shouldn't use them

Thus far, we have been using literals in many of our coding examples. It is time to recognize that literals usually are *not* the best way to represent a constant in a COBOL program. To illustrate our point, consider the following example:

```
MULTIPLY NUMBER-OF-GIZMOS TIMES 2.19
    GIVING TOTAL-GIZMO-PRICE.
```

By looking at this code, we deduce that the price of a single Gizmo is $2.19. However, it is highly likely that the price of a

Gizmo will change at some point in the near future. What will happen if we raise the price of a Gizmo to $2.99? We will have to hunt through the entire program looking for instances of the literal 2.19, and change each one to 2.99. As you might expect, several things can go wrong:

1.   We might overlook an instance of the literal 2.19 — and the boss will not be pleased when we underbill the client!

2.   While changing a literal from 2.19 to 2.99, we may have to repunch an entire COBOL state-ment — increasing the possibility that errors and bugs will be introduced into the program.

3.   We may inadvertently change a literal of 2.19 that had nothing to do with the price of Gizmos. It might turn out, for example, that the price of a Widget is also $2.19.

Far better programming style would be to define a field with the value of the current price of a Gizmo; we could then reference that field from any part of our program. For example, we might write

```
77  PRICE-PER-GIZMO          PIC 9V99  VALUE 2.19.
    ----------.
    ----------.
    ----------.
    MULTIPLY NUMBER-OF-GIZMOS
       TIMES PRICE-PER-GIZMO
       GIVING TOTAL-GIZMO-PRICE.
```

Now if the price changes, all we have to do is change the VALUE clause of the data definition. No instructions in the PROCEDURE DIVISION will have to be changed. With our Gizmo example, we would merely change the PIC definition as follows:

```
77  PRICE-PER-GIZMO          PIC 9V99  VALUE 2.99.
```

What we are saying, then, is that any change that is likely to occur should be accommodated by changing just one line of source program text, as we have done in the example above. Literal values are often used repeatedly in a program, and, as we pointed out earlier, they can be hard to spot when making modifications — *especially* when one is under a lot of pressure to fix a bug at 3:00 a.m. So, watch out for literals — and avoid them whenever you can.

9.6 The ALTER statement

In Chapter 8 we observed that the GO TO statement should be avoided if we wish to write *understandable* programs. Unfortunately, there is a statement that is even *worse* than the GO TO: the ALTER statement. It normally is used in conjunction with the GO TO statement to dynamically modify the paragraph-name to which the GO TO transfers control. Here is an example of an ALTER statement:

```
PROCEDURE DIVISION
       USING       CARD-AREA
                   CARD-EOF.
OPEN-BYPASS.
       GO TO OPEN-FILE.
OPEN-FILE.
       OPEN INPUT CARD-FILE.
       ALTER OPEN-BYPASS TO PROCEED TO READ-FILE.
READ-FILE.
       READ CARD-FILE INTO CARD-AREA
           AT END
               MOVE END-CARDS TO CARD-EOF
               CLOSE CARD-FILE.
EXIT-READ.
       EXIT PROGRAM.
```

As you can see, this program either OPENs and READs from a file of cards, or simply READs from the file, or READs and CLOSEs the file. The first time the program is CALLed, the file is OPENed, *and* the GO TO statement in OPEN-BYPASS is modified so that subsequent CALLs will skip around the OPEN-FILE paragraph and proceed directly to READ-FILE.

The GO TO statement, which serves as the object of the ALTER, must be in a paragraph by itself — the ALTER statement references the paragraph-name in which the GO TO resides. The GO TO cannot have a DEPENDING ON clause. Any number of ALTER statements may modify a single GO TO, as long as the ALTERs and the GO TO are in the same PROCEDURE DIVISION.

What's so horrible about the ALTER? It is nearly impossible to debug programs containing ALTER statements, because it makes a lie out of the program listing! Imagine, for example, that something has gone wrong with one of your programs. While debugging, you come across a statement that says

GO TO OPEN-FILE.

Naturally, you would innocently turn to paragraph OPEN-FILE and continue reading the code. But that is not what the GO TO "said" at *execution* time. Four pages after the GO TO statement, there is an ALTER lurking among some other statements . . . and it modified the GO TO statement to make control proceed to FORMAT-RECORD, which lies 15 pages away from OPEN-FILE. How long will it take you to discover that you are following the wrong trail?

The ALTER statement can cause so many debugging problems that many EDP organizations have banned its use completely. Chances are good that your programming group won't allow its use.[3] Even if your company allows its use, we strongly recommend that you avoid it. And even if you think you can handle an ALTER without getting personally confused, it eventually may cause problems for someone else — e.g., for the maintenance programmer who has to work with your programs several years after you've finished them. Indeed, if you discover an ALTER statement in an old program that you are maintaining, it is usually a good idea to remove it — *if* you can do so easily.

---

[3]Indeed, chances also are good that the American National Standards Institute (ANSI) soon will drop the ALTER statement from the official ANS definition of COBOL.

9.7 MOVE, ADD, and SUBTRACT CORRESPONDING

In all previous programming examples, we have given a unique name to every field of data — regardless of whether it was defined in the FILE SECTION, the WORKING-STORAGE SECTION, or the LINKAGE SECTION. Technically, we don't *have* to do it this way — and there are often good reasons for using the same field names in multiple structures of data. Consider the following example:

```
01   TAPE-IN.
     05   NAME              PIC      X(20).
     05   STREET-ADDR       PIC      X(30).
     05   CITY              PIC      X(15).
     05   STATE             PIC      X(2).
     05   ZIP-CODE          PIC      9(5).
----------.
----------.
----------.
01   PRINT-LINE.
     05   FILLER            PIC      X(2).
     05   NAME              PIC      X(20).
     05   FILLER            PIC      X(10).
     05   STREET-ADDR       PIC      X(30)
     05   FILLER            PIC      X(10).
     05   CITY              PIC      X(15).
     05   FILLER            PIC      X(10).
     05   STATE             PIC      X(2).
     05   FILLER            PIC      X(10).
     05   ZIP-CODE          PIC      9(5).
     05   FILLER            PIC      X(18).
----------.
----------.
----------.
MOVE NAME IN TAPE-IN
     TO NAME IN PRINT-LINE.
----------.
----------.
----------.
```

Different fields defined with the same name are called *qualified data-names*. In order to refer to a nonunique data-name, we must give not only the data-name but also the group name of the group item to which it belongs. The group name *must* be unique; however, the group name does not have to be the immediately superior level to the data-name that is being qualified. The following code illustrates this point:

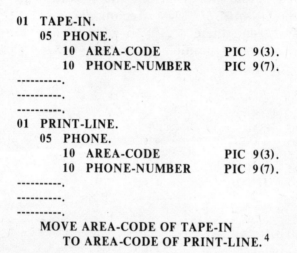

```
01  TAPE-IN.
    05  PHONE.
        10  AREA-CODE        PIC 9(3).
        10  PHONE-NUMBER     PIC 9(7).
----------.
----------.
----------.
01  PRINT-LINE.
    05  PHONE.
        10  AREA-CODE        PIC 9(3).
        10  PHONE-NUMBER     PIC 9(7).
----------.
----------.
----------.
        MOVE AREA-CODE OF TAPE-IN
          TO AREA-CODE OF PRINT-LINE.[4]
```

When working with qualified data-names, we can move them one at a time:

```
        MOVE NAME OF TAPE-IN
          TO NAME OF PRINT-LINE.
        MOVE STREET-ADDR OF TAPE-IN
          TO STREET-ADDR OF PRINT-LINE.
        MOVE CITY OF TAPE-IN
          TO CITY OF PRINT-LINE.
----------.
----------.
----------.
```

---

[4]In COBOL, we can use either the key word OF or the key word IN when describing a qualified data reference.

Or, we can move them all at once:

MOVE CORRESPONDING TAPE-IN TO PRINT-LINE.

The MOVE CORRESPONDING statement will MOVE every elementary data field — a field defined with type and length, e.g., X(6) — to another field with the same data-name, providing that the qualification of the fields is identical to, but *not* including, the group names stated in the MOVE CORRESPONDING. Fields meeting this criterion will not be moved if they contain a RENAMES, REDEFINES, or OCCURS clause. Don't worry about this at the moment — we'll examine those clauses in the next two chapters.

Besides moving fields, we can also ADD CORRESPONDING or SUBTRACT CORRESPONDING. The rules are the same whether we MOVE, ADD, or SUBTRACT with the CORRESPONDING clause. Here's an example of ADD CORRESPONDING:

```
05   CUSTOMER-BALANCE.
     10   DUE-LAST-MONTH      PIC    9(5)V99.
     10   DUE-THIS-MONTH      PIC    9(5)V99.
     10   PAID-LAST-MONTH     PIC    9(5)V99.
----------.
----------.
----------.
05   TOTAL-MONTHLY-BALANCE.
     10   DUE-LAST-MONTH      PIC    9(6)V99.
     10   PAID-LAST-MONTH     PIC    9(6)V99.
     10   DUE-THIS-MONTH      PIC    9(6)V99.
----------.
----------.
----------.
ADD CORRESPONDING CUSTOMER-BALANCE
    TO TOTAL-MONTHLY-BALANCE.
----------.
----------.
----------.
```

Notice that the elementary items are not in the same order in the two group items shown above. That's perfectly acceptable. Also, note that the receiving fields are larger than the sending fields. That's all right, too, since the ADD CORRESPONDING statement will behave as if we had written the following code:

```
ADD DUE-LAST-MONTH OF CUSTOMER-BALANCE
   TO DUE-LAST-MONTH OF TOTAL-MONTHLY-BALANCE.
ADD PAID-LAST-MONTH OF CUSTOMER-BALANCE
   TO PAID-LAST-MONTH OF TOTAL-MONTHLY-BALANCE.
ADD DUE-THIS-MONTH OF CUSTOMER-BALANCE
   TO DUE-THIS-MONTH OF TOTAL-MONTHLY-BALANCE.
-----------.
-----------.
-----------.
```

The MOVE, ADD, and SUBTRACT CORRESPONDING statements look pretty handy, don't they? *Wrong!* One of the most frequently changed parts of a program is the format of input records and output records. When such record definitions change, it is very easy to foul up the requirements for the CORRESPONDING clause. In the long run, it is better to use the straightforward MOVE, ADD, and SUBTRACT statements. They explicitly state what is happening, and, therefore, are significantly easier to follow.

9.8 The COMPUTE statement

Occasionally, you'll find that the simple ADD, SUBTRACT, MULTIPLY, and DIVIDE statements are not sufficient to easily express a computation. For example, we could write

```
MULTIPLY SIDE BY SIDE
   GIVING SQUARE-FEET.
```

but it would be more convenient to use the *exponentiation* (raising a number to a power) operator ``**'' and the COMPUTE statement to do the same thing:

```
COMPUTE SQUARE-FEET = SIDE ** 2.
```

The COMPUTE statement should be used whenever a computation is sufficiently complicated that it would be excessively verbose to express with ADDs, MULTIPLYs, and so forth. Similarly, the COMPUTE statement should be used whenever a well-known formula is to be invoked or exponentiation is required. Incidentally, we can even use the COMPUTE statement to determine *roots* of a number:

COMPUTE SIDE = SQUARE-FEET ** 0.5.

We now have seen the complete set of arithmetic operators: i.e., +, −, *, /, and **. However, there is one topic that remains to be discussed: the *precedence* of these arithmetic operators. For example, how would the COBOL compiler interpret the following statement?

COMPUTE A = +9/4 * E + F ** 3 − C.

The first operation is to make the 9 a "+9". This is called unary arithmetic − simply making "plus" numbers positive, and "minus" numbers negative. The next operation performed is exponentiation: F is to be raised to the third power. The next lower "precedence" is division and multiplication, both of which have the same level of "binding." [Remember the commutative law of arithmetic? A*(B/C) is the same as (A*B)/C.]

Since multiplication and division are at the same level, the compiler works from left to right on the COBOL statement that it is analyzing. Thus, the expression 9/4 is resolved, and the result is then multiplied by E. Next come addition and subtraction, which operate at the same level of precedence. Consequently, addition and subtraction are carried out in a left-to-right fashion; so, the expression (+9/4)*E is added to the expression F**3, and C is then subtracted.

To generalize from this example, we can see that the order − or precedence − of arithmetic operations is as follows:

first	unary arithmetic operators
second	exponentiation
third	multiplication, division (performed left to right)
fourth	addition, subtraction (performed left to right)

An important, additional point should be made: Even though the COBOL compiler *knows* the order in which computations should be carried out, you should act as if it doesn't. Why? Because our biggest problem is writing programs that can be understood by people. Imagine your dilemma if you were a maintenance programmer desperately trying to find a bug at 3:00 a.m., and you narrowed the bug down to the general vicinity of the following statement:

$$COMPUTE\ A\ =\ +9/4\ *\ E\ +\ F\ **\ 3\ -\ C.$$

Naturally, you would begin to wonder (a) if your memory of the precedence of exponentiation, multiplication, and addition were correct, (b) if there were a bug in the COBOL compiler, and (c) whether the original programmer really knew the order in which the computations were to be carried out. How much better it would have been had the original programmer simply written

$$COMPUTE\ A\ =\ ((+9/4)\ *\ E)\ +\ (F\ **\ 3)\ -\ C.$$

In addition to the strong argument of readability, there is another practical reason for using parentheses liberally in a COMPUTE statement: Doing so allows us to change the order of computation so that the compiler will work from the innermost parentheses outward. For example, parentheses are *extremely* desirable — and absolutely necessary — in a COBOL statement such as the following:

$$COMPUTE\ BALANCE\text{-}DUE\ =$$
$$(TOTAL\text{-}DUE\ -\ LAST\text{-}PAYMENT)\ /\ MONTHS\text{-}REMAINING.\ [5]$$

---

[5]Note that the presence of a "space" character changes the meaning of the "-" character from a "hyphen" to a "minus."

If we are carrying out a complex computation, it is better programming style to break the COMPUTE down into a series of smaller COMPUTEs, introducing *meaningful* data-names to hold intermediate results. For example, suppose we were required to calculate the minimum payment for a credit card holder. Let's assume that the minimum payment is defined as 10 percent of the outstanding balance, where outstanding balance is defined as last month's balance minus last month's payment, plus 1 percent interest on that outstanding amount, plus any new charges. We could write the following code:

```
COMPUTE THIS-MONTH-BALANCE =
   (((LAST-MONTH-BALANCE – PAYMENT) * INTEREST)
   + NEW-CHARGES) / NUMBER-OF-PAYMENTS.
```

but it would be far more understandable if we wrote

```
COMPUTE OUTSTANDING-BALANCE =
   (LAST-MONTH-BALANCE – PAYMENT) * INTEREST.
COMPUTE TOTAL-DUE =
   OUTSTANDING-BALANCE + NEW-CHARGES.
COMPUTE THIS-MONTH-BALANCE =
   TOTAL-DUE / NUMBER-OF-PAYMENTS.
```

As always, readability is the most important consideration. The COMPUTE statement can either aid or hinder the understandability of your program, depending on how it is used.

9.9 The INSPECT/EXAMINE statement

This book is based on the version of COBOL defined by the American National Standards Institute in 1974 — otherwise known as 1974 ANS COBOL. The American National Standards Institute previously defined a standard version of COBOL in 1968. Today, many COBOL compilers still adhere to the 1968 standards, rather than the 1974 standards.

One of the major differences between the 1968 and 1974 versions of COBOL is the elimination of the EXAMINE statement (from 1968 ANS COBOL) and the addition of the more flexible INSPECT statement. If your COBOL compiler is based on the 1968 standards, you will have to use the EXAMINE statement because the INSPECT statement will not be recognized. Both instructions are useful for counting and/or replacing characters in a string of data.

To illustrate the use of the INSPECT/EXAMINE statements, suppose we want to write a program to read cards that describe the amount of money owed to us by our clients. Let's assume that the card has a five-position field for the amount of money. However, the keypunch operators have been told that they do not have to keypunch leading zeroes if the amount occupies four or fewer positions. Thus, we might have a card that looks like the following:

bb295

(Note that we have used the character "**b**" to represent the "blank" character.) Before we can do any arithmetic with this number, we must make it purely numeric. The following statements will do the trick:

**EXAMINE CLIENT-BALANCE
REPLACING LEADING SPACES BY ZEROS.**

or

**INSPECT CLIENT-BALANCE
REPLACING LEADING SPACES BY ZEROES.**

(Note that COBOL accepts both ZEROS and ZEROES as the plural for ZERO. For the sake of consistency, pick one spelling and stick with it.) The result of this operation can be summarized with the following example:

BEFORE	AFTER
bb295	00295

Not only can we replace LEADING characters, but we also can use the EXAMINE statement to replace ALL, FIRST, and UNTIL FIRST. Here's an example:

FIELD-A BEFORE	COBOL STATEMENT	FIELD-A AFTER
bb2b7b	**EXAMINE FIELD-A** **REPLACING ALL SPACES BY ZEROES.**	002070
bb2b7b	**EXAMINE FIELD-A** **REPLACING UNTIL FIRST '7' BY '3'.**	33337b

The INSPECT can do whatever the EXAMINE can do, plus much more. Not only can we replace characters before the first occurrence of a specified character, but also after the specified character. For example:

FIELD-A BEFORE	COBOL STATEMENT	FIELD-A AFTER
bb2b7b	**INSPECT FIELD-A** **REPLACING CHARACTERS BY ZEROES** **AFTER INITIAL '2'.**	bb2000
bbbb1111	**INSPECT FIELD-A** **REPLACING CHARACTERS BY ZEROES** **BEFORE INITIAL '1'.**	00001111
ESEZINP	**INSPECT FIELD-A** **REPLACING ALL 'E' BY 'A', 'S' BY 'M',** **'P' BY 'G'.**	AMAZING

In addition to using INSPECT and EXAMINE to replace characters, you can also count characters. There is a special field called TALLY, defined by and known to the COBOL compiler. This field is the repository of the count when you use either the INSPECT or the EXAMINE statement. You don't have to define TALLY in your DATA DIVISION; it is defined automatically as a 9(5) item, as shown on the following page:

BEFORE	COBOL STATEMENT	AFTER	TALLY
002107	EXAMINE FIELD-A TALLYING ALL ZEROES.	002107	3
002107	INSPECT FIELD-A TALLYING ALL '1'.	002107	1

After either of these instructions, you may reference TALLY as you would any other field. For example:

IF TALLY GREATER THAN ZERO . . .

or

ADD TALLY TO ZERO-COUNT.

You can even count and replace characters simultaneously, as the following example illustrates:

BEFORE	COBOL STATEMENT	AFTER	TALLY

bbb322	EXAMINE FIELD-A
	    TALLYING LEADING SPACES
	    REPLACING BY ZEROES.
		000322	3

or

0064.22	INSPECT FIELD-A
	    TALLYING ZERO-COUNT
	    FOR LEADING ZEROES
	    REPLACING ALL '.' BY ZERO.
		0064022	ZERO-
			COUNT=2

Notice that the INSPECT in the example above included the clause TALLYING ZERO-COUNT. When counting with the INSPECT statement, we can have the TALLY count placed in any field we wish, provided we define the field as a numeric elementary item.

Thus, we might define ZERO-COUNT as follows:

        77 ZERO-COUNT   PIC 9(2).

Unfortunately, this particular feature is not available with the EX-AMINE statement.

    Both the EXAMINE and the INSPECT statements are very powerful and have a myriad of options. Whether you use the 1968 EXAMINE statement, or the 1974 INSPECT statement, you should take a look at all of the possibilities in your COBOL manual. One or two common uses of INSPECT/EXAMINE should probably be made part of your standard repertory of programming tools.

    Following are a few problems for you to try. For each coding example, describe the effect on the test-field and on TALLY. The answers can be found in the Appendix.

BEFORE   COBOL STATEMENT   AFTER   TALLY

b1274   EXAMINE TEST-FIELD
                TALLYING UNTIL FIRST '4'
                REPLACING BY SPACE.

BANANA   EXAMINE TEST-FIELD
                REPLACING ALL 'A' BY 'E'.

b$1346   INSPECT TEST-FIELD
                TALLYING NUMB-COUNT
                FOR CHARACTERS AFTER INITIAL '$'
                REPLACING FIRST '$' BY SPACE.

ELEMENT   INSPECT TEST-FIELD
                REPLACING ALL 'LE' BY 'DA',
                FIRST 'E' BY 'Q'.

9.10 The STRING/UNSTRING statement

We have seen how we can use the MOVE CORRESPONDING statement to copy elementary items of one group into their counterparts in another group. The STRING statement is, in a sense, the opposite of MOVE CORRESPONDING. That is, the STRING statement can be thought of as a move *not* corresponding. The STRING statement can accept fields from diverse sources and order them, one after another, into an elementary alphanumeric data item. This sounds as if it is just another way of disguising a series of simple MOVEs, but the STRING statement has some features which go well beyond that.

Suppose, for example, that we had to write a CALLable program which would format a "detail" line for subsequent printing. Our program will receive a client-record, a balance-due field, and a flag representing the client's billing status. It eventually will call a subordinate module, PRINTCL,[6] passing it a formatted print-line to be written. The piece of the structure chart that we are working on looks like this:

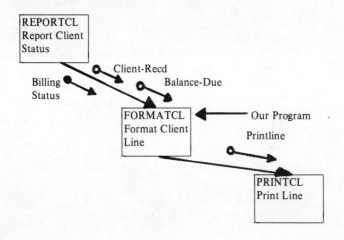

---

[6]Unfortunately, most implementations of COBOL allow a maximum of eight alphanumeric characters for a program name. Thus, CALLed programs often have non-mnemonic names.

When this program is CALLed once, the print-line passed to PRINTCL should contain this information:

MR. S. SPADE 44221 21 W. 43 ST. NY NY 10036 2140.83 (0 — STATUS *) 60 DAYS IN ARREARS, SEND LETTER

We might imagine that the "0" status means that the client's bill is 60 days in arrears, and that he should be sent a letter.

```
IDENTIFICATION DIVISION.
PROGRAM-ID. FORMATCL.

ENVIRONMENT DIVISION.

DATA DIVISION.

WORKING-STORAGE SECTION.

01   BEST-MSG                PIC X(11)       VALUE 'A1-STATUS *'.
01   OKAY-MSG                PIC X(10)       VALUE 'C-STATUS *'.
01   BAD-MSG                 PIC X(10)       VALUE '0-STATUS *'.
01   END-OF-STATUS           PIC X           VALUE '*'.
01   STATUS-MSG              PIC X(11).
01   1ST-WARNING             PIC X(26)
                             VALUE 'NOTIFY 30 DAYS IN ARREARS-'.
01   2ND-WARNING             PIC X(32)
                             VALUE '60 DAYS IN ARREARS, SEND LETTER-'.
01   ATTORNEY-MSG            PIC X(31)
                             VALUE '90 DAYS LATE, NOTIFY ATTORNEYS-'.
01   END-OF-ACTION           PIC X           VALUE '-'.
01   ACTION-TO-TAKE          PIC X(32).
01   PRINTLINE               PIC X(132).
01   NORMAL-INDENT           PIC 9(3)        VALUE 5.
01   BLANK-3                 PIC X(3)        VALUE SPACES.
01   BLANK-5                 PIC X(5)        VALUE SPACES.

LINKAGE SECTION.
01   CLIENT-RECORD.
     05   CLIENT-NAME        PIC X(20).
     05   CLIENT-NUMBER      PIC 9(5).
     05   CLIENT-ADDR        PIC X(30).
     05   CLIENT-ZIP         PIC 9(5).
     05   CLIENT-STATUS      PIC 9.
          88   EXCELLENT-STATUS                VALUE 1.
          88   OKAY-STATUS                     VALUE 2.
          88   POOR-STATUS                     VALUE 3.

01   BALANCE-DUE             PIC 9(4)V99.

01   BILLING-STATUS          PIC 9(2).
          88   30-DAYS-LATE                    VALUE 30.
```

```
          88    60-DAYS-LATE                    VALUE 60.
          88    90-DAYS-LATE                    VALUE 90.
EJECT


* FORMATCL IS A PROGRAM CALLED BY REPORTST WHICH FORMATS A
* PRINTLINE DEPENDING ON THE BILLING STATUS INDICATOR.
* IT PASSES THE PRINTLINE ONTO 'PRINTCL' TO HANDLE WRITING

PROCEDURE DIVISION
     USING                      CLIENT-RECORD
                                BALANCE-DUE
                                BILLING-STATUS.

CHECK-STATUS.
     IF EXCELLENT-STATUS
          MOVE BEST-MSG TO STATUS-MSG
     ELSE IF OKAY-STATUS
          MOVE OKAY-MSG TO STATUS-MSG
     ELSE IF POOR-STATUS
          MOVE BAD-MSG TO STATUS MSG.

     IF 30-DAYS-LATE
          MOVE 1ST-WARNING TO ACTION-TO-TAKE
     ELSE IF 60-DAYS-LATE
          MOVE 2ND-WARNING TO ACTION-TO-TAKE
     ELSE
          MOVE ATTORNEY-MSG TO ACTION-TO-TAKE.
     MOVE SPACES TO PRINTLINE.
          STRING
          CLIENT-NAME DELIMITED BY SIZE

          CLIENT-NUMBER DELIMITED BY SIZE
          BLANK-3 DELIMITED BY SIZE
          CLIENT-ADDR DELIMITED BY SIZE

          CLIENT-ZIP DELIMITED BY SIZE
          BLANK-5 DELIMITED BY SIZE
          BALANCE-DUE DELIMITED BY SIZE

          STATUS-MSG DELIMITED BY END-OF-STATUS
          ACTION-TO-TAKE DELIMITED BY END-OF-ACTION
     INTO PRINTLINE
          WITH POINTER NORMAL-INDENT.

     CALL 'PRINTCL' USING PRINTLINE.

EXIT-FORMATCL.
     EXIT PROGRAM.
```

The STRING statement works left to right on the receiving field. For example, the INTO PRINTLINE WITH POINTER clause directs the ordering of fields — and it indicates that we should begin with the fifth position of the line. If we had omitted this clause, then "stringing" would begin in the first position of the line. The size of the field acting as a pointer must be large enough to hold the length of the receiving field *plus one*. The length of PRINTLINE is 132, so (length of PRINTLINE) + 1 is 133 — thus, the pointer is defined as a three-position field. Each field is listed in the order in which it is to be placed on the line.

The DELIMITED BY SIZE clause means that the entire field should be moved. If we wish, we can move just a part of a field. For example, STATUS-MSG is DELIMITED BY END-OF-STATUS, which has a value of '*'. This tells the STRING statement to move only that part of the field which is to the left of the *first* occurrence of an asterisk.

As you can see, STRING is most useful when packing a series of items into a linear sequence. It helps us to avoid writing many MOVEs and, more important, to avoid writing complex record layouts for output lines. All of the complexity is kept in one place: in the STRING statement itself.

The UNSTRING statement takes an elementary alphanumeric data item as its input, and moves data from that alphanumeric data item to separate fields. The fields can be defined as numeric, alphanumeric, or alphabetic data items. The UNSTRING statement is used most often in reformatting raw input so that each field may be edited.

To illustrate the UNSTRING statement, suppose we want to write a CALLed program that will build a charge card record for billing a commercial airline flight. The input to the program is a card in the following format: charge number/from airport/to airport/flight number/number of seats/coach or first class/ departure date/. For example, both of the following two cards are valid:

    00427689757100AX/JFK/LAX/10/7/C/012177/
    38180056290006DC/LAG/LGN/351/3/F/022777/

The card that follows is invalid because it has too few fields:

    00476972237686AX/SFO/ATL/222/3/C/

The output returned to the CALLing program follows:

```
00427689757100AX 012177 JFK LAX 10b 1bbC 3818005629000bDC 022277 LAG LGN 351
3bbF
```

We are not supposed to edit the field — all we have to do is re-
format the input field into the kind of output shown above. If
any field is missing, or if there are extra fields, we should print
the entire card, and an error message — which will be accomplished by CALLing a program known as ERROROUT, which expects the entire card and an appropriate message.

```
IDENTIFICATION DIVISION
PROGRAM-ID. BUILDREC.

ENVIRONMENT DIVISION.

DATA DIVISION.

WORKING-STORAGE SECTION.

01    CARD-AREA            PIC X(80).
01    END-OF-CARDS         PIC X(3)   VALUE SPACES.
01    NUMBER-OF-FIELDS     PIC 9.
01    TOO-MANY-FIELDS      PIC X(3).
01    MARKER               PIC X      VALUE '/'.
01    PROPER-NUMBER        PIC 9      VALUE 7.
01    TOO-MANY-MSG         PIC X(24)  VALUE 'REJECTED TOO MANY FIELDS'.
01    TOO-FEW-MSG          PIC X(24)  VALUE 'REJECTED TOO FEW FIELDS '.

LINKAGE SECTION.

01    CHARGE-RECORD.
      05    CHARGE-CODE     PIC X(16).
      05    DEPART-DATE     PIC X(6).
      05    FROM-AIRPORT    PIC X(3).
      05    TO-AIRPORT      PIC X(3).
      05    FLIGHT-NUMBER   PIC X(3).
      05    NUMBER-OF-SEATS PIC X(3).
      05    FIRST-OR-COACH  PIC X.
01    EOF-RECORDS          PIC X(3).
* THIS PROGRAM, CALLED BY EDITREC, FORMATS A CARD ACCORDING TO THE
* LAYOUT OF CHARGE-RECORD. IF FIELDS ARE MISSING OR THERE IS EXTRA
* DATA, THE CARD IS REJECTED AND 'ERROROUT' IS CALLED. IT GETS A CARD
* BY CALLING 'GETCARD'.

PROCEDURE DIVISION
      USING    CHARGE-RECORD
               EOF-RECORDS.
REFORMAT.
      MOVE ZEROES TO NUMBER-OF-FIELDS.
      CALL 'GETCARD'
        USING CARD-AREA
              END-OF-CARDS.

      PERFORM REFORMAT-LOOP
        UNTIL END-OF-CARDS = 'YES'
           OR NUMBER-OF-FIELDS = PROPER-NUMBER.
      IF END-OF-CARDS = 'YES'
        MOVE 'YES' TO EOF-RECORDS.
REFORMAT-EXIT.
      EXIT PROGRAM.
```

```
REFORMAT-LOOP.
    MOVE 'NO' TO TOO-MANY-FIELDS.
    MOVE ZEROES TO NUMBER-OF-FIELDS.

    UNSTRING
    CARD-AREA DELIMITED BY MARKER
        INTO CHARGE-CODE
            FROM-AIRPORT
            TO-AIRPORT
            FLIGHT-NUMBER
            NUMBER-OF-SEATS
            FIRST-OR-COACH
            DEPART-DATE
        TALLYING IN NUMBER-OF-FIELDS
    ON OVERFLOW MOVE 'YES' TO TOO-MANY-FIELDS.

    IF TOO-MANY-FIELDS = 'YES'
        CALL 'ERROROUT'
            USING    CARD-AREA
                     TOO-MANY-MSG
        CALL 'GETCARD'
            USING    CARD-AREA
                     END-OF-CARDS
    ELSE IF NUMBER-OF-FIELDS LESS THAN PROPER-NUMBER
        CALL 'ERROROUT'
            USING    CARD-AREA
                     TOO-FEW-MSG
        CALL 'GETCARD'
            USING    CARD-AREA
                     END-OF-CARDS.
```

Note that the UNSTRING statement in the code above strips off the fields delimited by a '/'. It also keeps count of the number of fields it has moved in NUMBER-OF-FIELDS. If there should be more fields on the card and the receiving fields have all been used, the UNSTRING statement will carry out the actions specified by the ON OVERFLOW clause. Similarly, the ON OVERFLOW clause is normally used with the STRING statement for occasions when the receiving field may be too small to hold all the fields.

We have shown a relatively simple example of the UN-STRING statement. The UNSTRING, like the STRING, can have a WITH POINTER clause, and can count the number of positions moved into any receiving field. These facilities will enable you to perform many useful operations, but you may wish to refer to your COBOL language manual for other uses of this sophisticated instruction.

9.11 The ACCEPT/DISPLAY statement

The DISPLAY statement normally is used to output a small message — usually to the computer operator. For example, one might write the following statement:

**DISPLAY 'INVALID MASTER FOUND, ACCOUNT-' MSTR-ACCOUNT
  UPON CONSOLE.**

The coding above causes the literal and a master record account number to be DISPLAYed. Literals are DISPLAYed by enclosing them in single quotes; the contents of various fields can be DISPLAYed by listing the field-name in the DISPLAY statement. The UPON CONSOLE clause will send the message to the computer operator's console terminal (which almost always is located in the computer room, right next to the tapes, disks, printers, and CPU). Messages can also be DISPLAYed upon any other device that is normally used to receive output data; to do this, merely write UPON "device-name" instead of UPON CONSOLE. Device-name must be specified in the SPECIAL-NAMES paragraph of the ENVIRONMENT DIVISION.

The 1974 ANS COBOL standards permit you to obtain the date, day, and time of day by using the ACCEPT statement. For example, one might write

ACCEPT TODAY-DATE FROM DATE.

DATE is an internally defined field — like TALLY; you need not worry about defining it in your DATA DIVISION. In effect, it is a 9(6) item, in the format YYMMDD. Thus, July 4, 1976 would be represented as 760704.

The ACCEPT statement also can be used to input small amounts of data — typically, from the operator's console terminal, or some other on-line typewriter. We might write the following code:

```
MOVE SPACES TO REPORT-ANSWER.
DISPLAY 'SUMMARY REPORT TO BE PRINTED?
    - REPLY Y OR N'.
PERFORM GET-ANSWER
    UNTIL REPORT-ANSWER = 'Y'
        OR REPORT-ANSWER = 'N'.
    ----------.
    ----------.
    ----------.
GET-ANSWER.
    ACCEPT REPORT-ANSWER FROM CONSOLE.
    IF REPORT-ANSWER NOT EQUAL 'Y'
        AND REPORT-ANSWER NOT EQUAL TO 'N'
        DISPLAY 'SUMMARY REPORT TO BE PRINTED?
            - REPLY Y OR N'.
```

Because their use is extremely implementation-dependent, ACCEPT and DISPLAY should be used sparingly, if at all. It is best to hide them in CALLed modules, so that only the module need change when a program is moved from one environment to another. Indeed, some EDP organizations have banned the use of ACCEPT and DISPLAY in order to ensure the portability of COBOL programs from one computer environment to another.

9.12 The STOP RUN statement

The STOP RUN statement will cause a program to return to the operating system. Only the topmost module in a hierarchy of modules should have a STOP RUN statement; ideally, it should be the physically last statement of the top-level module. All other modules (i.e., CALLed subprograms) should have an EXIT PRO-GRAM statement to cause them to return to the CALLing program. This is an important point: If a low-level module (which has been CALLed by a module, which was CALLed by some other module, which was CALLed by some other module, and so forth) should execute a STOP RUN statement, then the entire hierarchy of modules will exit to the operating system. Since we want all modules to have a single entry point and a single exit, we would expect to have only one STOP RUN or EXIT PROGRAM statement per program.

10 Internal Coding and the DATA DIVISION

10.1 Representing numbers with ones and zeroes

If someone asked you, "What was the largest number of home runs hit in one season by a major league baseball player?" how would you respond? Assuming that you knew, you would answer, "61." Without even thinking about it, we naturally express numerical quantities as base ten numbers. Thus, 61 is convenient shorthand for 6 tens and 1 one. If, instead, we assumed that 61 were a base seven number (written as 61_7), then 61 would be equivalent to 6 sevens and 1 one — or 43_{10}.

When dealing with computers, the basic unit of information is the bit, which is a binary, or base two, digit. When representing binary numbers, only 1's and 0's are valid digits. The following example illustrates this:

$$
\begin{array}{rcrcl}
101101_2 & = & 1 \times 2^5 & = & 32 \\
& & + \ 0 \times 2^4 & = & 0 \\
& & + \ 1 \times 2^3 & = & 8 \\
& & + \ 1 \times 2^2 & = & 4 \\
& & + \ 0 \times 2^1 & = & 0 \\
& & + \ 1 \times 2^0 & = & 1 \\
& & & & \overline{} \\
& & & & 45_{10}
\end{array}
$$

When dealing with long strings of bits (they grow in length more rapidly than decimal numbers), it is easier to represent them as hexadecimal, or base 16, numbers. Since 16 is equal to 2^4, each hexadecimal digit summarizes four bits of information: A number expressed by 12 binary digits could be expressed in three hexadecimal digits. When writing hexadecimal numbers, 0 through 9 have the same value as 0 through 9 in the base ten system; the letters A through F are used to signify values of ten through 15. For example:

$$3D = (3 \times 16) + (13 \times 1) = 61_{10}$$

A four-position binary field has 16 possible values, from 0000 (0_{16}), to 1111 (F_{16}). To convert any binary number to its hexadecimal equivalent, work from right to left, grouping four bits at a time. For example:

C90B8785

1100 1001 0000 1011 1000 0111 1000 0101

In most computers, the next unit of information after the bit is the byte. The number of bits within a byte varies from vendor to vendor. Most machines are designed eight bits to the byte, but some have six- or nine-bit bytes. Assuming that you have an eight-bit per byte machine, what is the largest number — in base 16 — that a byte can contain?

$$1111\ 1111_2 = FF_{16} = 255_{10}$$

The byte is the basic unit of internal storage for holding data. When we define data — e.g., an elementary item in WORKING-STORAGE — the size of the internal storage needed to hold that item is computed in terms of bytes.

10.2 Representing characters: USAGE DISPLAY, COMP, COMP-3

There are several forms we can use to represent byte-oriented information. The simplest form is *numeric character,* in which one byte contains one character. Numeric character format is known as DISPLAY in COBOL. It is the only way we can store non-numeric data — e.g., alphabetic strings such as ABC, or alphanumeric strings such as A97B. Indeed, we have been using the DISPLAY form exclusively in this book; it is the default form when defining data. Thus,

      01 CUSTOMER-STATE   PIC XX.
      01 CUSTOMER-STATE   PIC XX
          USAGE DISPLAY.

define CUSTOMER-STATE in exactly the same way; both define a two-character field to hold a two-letter state code.

With the DISPLAY format, each number, letter, or special character (e.g., "$", ".", ",", or "+") is assigned a unique eight-bit binary value, that is, a unique byte value. The most popular system for representing the character codes is known as EBCDIC — an acronym for Extended Binary Coded Decimal Interchange Code. The other popular coding scheme is known as ASCII, which is an acronym for American Standard Code for Information Interchange. We will use EBCDIC code, shown in Table 10.1 on the following page.

Note that we show the characters in ascending order of binary value. This is called the *collating sequence;* it determines the result when we compare one field with another — i.e., the binary value of 3 is less than the binary value of 4.

To illustrate the use of DISPLAY, suppose we define the following field:

      01 PRESIDENT   PIC X(6)   VALUE 'CARTER'.

The six-position field, with the value CARTER, would be expressed as the following hexadecimal quantity:

Table 10.1. Letters and Numbers in EBCDIC.

Binary Value	Hexadecimal Value	Character
1100 0001	C1	A
1100 0010	C2	B
1100 0011	C3	C
1100 0100	C4	D
1100 0101	C5	E
1100 0110	C6	F
1100 0111	C7	G
1100 1000	C8	H
1100 1001	C9	I
1101 0010	D1	J
1101 0011	D2	K
1101 0011	D3	L
1101 0100	D4	M
1101 0101	D5	N
1101 0110	D6	O
1101 0111	D7	P
1101 1000	D8	Q
1101 1010	D9	R
1110 0010	E2	S
1110 0011	E3	T
1110 0100	E4	U
1110 0101	E5	V
1110 0110	E6	W
1110 0111	E7	X
1110 1000	E8	Y
1110 1001	E9	Z
1111 0000	F0	0
1111 0001	F1	1
1111 0010	F2	2
1111 0011	F3	3
1111 0100	F4	4
1111 0101	F5	5
1111 0110	F6	6
1111 0111	F7	7
1111 1000	F8	8
1111 1001	F9	9

When we define any numeric field with the DISPLAY format, it is important to remember that the sign is carried somewhere within the confines of the number, not as a separate character. Notice in Table 10.1 that the digits 0 through 9 are represented as hexadecimal F0 through F9. The four bits comprising the F are called *zone bits,* while the four bits which describe the integer are called *numeric bits* (thus the *numeric* format we mentioned earlier). Different vendors hold the sign of numeric fields in different locations, but all vendors include the sign within the number itself. In the IBM 360/370 series, when a number is defined as a positive quantity, the zone bits of the low-order digit will be a hexadecimal C instead of an F; if the number is negative, the low-order zone bits will be a D. For example, the COBOL statement

01   DEDUCTION   PIC S9(4)   VALUE   +1500.

would cause DEDUCTION to be stored internally in the following format:

| F1 | F5 | F0 | C0 |

In the programs and the examples we have seen thus far, we did arithmetic — ADD, SUBTRACT, MULTIPLY, DIVIDE, and COMPUTE — with numeric fields in DISPLAY form. When we do arithmetic with DISPLAY fields, the fields are usually converted to another format before the calculations actually take place. For IBM COBOL, arithmetic always is done on fields in *packed decimal* format. IBM COBOL's name for packed decimal is COMP-3, which is an abbreviation for COMPUTATIONAL-3.[1] In the COMP-3 format, the zone bits are dropped — so that two numeric digits can be held in one eight-bit byte. In order to preserve the sign of the number, the low-order sign byte of the DISPLAY form has its zone and numeric bits reversed when converting to the COMP-3 format.

---

[1] COMP-3 is actually a vendor name. Packed decimal is not defined in the ANSI COBOL standards.

For example, the data item DEDUCTION introduced above could be represented in either of the following two forms:

DEDUCTION as DISPLAY   DEDUCTION as COMP-3

| F1F5F0C0 | | 01500C |

We have packed four bytes of DISPLAY data into three bytes of COMP-3 data. Obviously, the saving in memory is greater if we are dealing with longer numbers — it can be as much as 50 percent. Note also that a high-order zero was added to the COMP-3 form of DEDUCTION; this is done automatically by COBOL, since (on almost all computers) each data item must begin and end on a byte boundary.

It is simple to define COMP-3 fields in the WORKING-STORAGE SECTION of our program. For example:

01   P1   PIC S9V9999   VALUE   +3.1426   USAGE COMP-3.

or

01   P1   PIC S9V9999   VALUE   +3.1426   COMP-3.

In this example, we still define the field in terms of the number of positions needed to express it as a decimal quantity. That is, the PIC clause must indicate that P1 is a numeric item that requires five decimal digits and a decimal point. When defining the data, we do not worry about the number of bytes that will be used to hold the number internally in the computer.

With IBM COBOL, use the COMP-3 format on all fields that are defined by the programmer, and intended for use in arithmetic statements. By defining fields in this fashion, we avoid the time-consuming conversion from DISPLAY to COMP-3, which otherwise would take place every time the DISPLAY field was referenced in an arithmetic statement.

There is a third format for holding numeric data. It is
known as COMP, and is used to represent data in a binary form.
The COMP format requires that the field be either two bytes (i.e.,
a half-word on computers such as the IBM System/370), or four
bytes (a full word on the IBM System/360). Of the 16 bits that
are available in a two-byte quantity, 15 are used to represent the
number, and one is used to indicate the sign. Thus, such
numbers must be in the range $\pm 32767_{10}$. Normally, we use
COMP numbers in COBOL to do arithmetic when using non-IBM
COBOL compilers, and to describe subscripts and indexes for all
compilers. Subscripts and indexes are discussed in Chapter 11.

10.3 Alignment of fields: SYNC, JUSTIFIED

When we work with binary (COMP) fields, we must ensure
that they are always aligned on an internal computer boundary.
Every byte of internal storage has a unique *address* — that is, a
number that describes a specific position in the internal storage
area (or memory) of the computer. Most computers that run
COBOL programs have millions of such bytes of internal storage.

With IBM COBOL, every half-word (i.e., a two-byte quantity) must begin on a *half-word boundary;* that is, the left-most
byte of the pair must have an address that is divisible by two.
Similarly, full-word binary fields must be aligned in such a way
that the left-most byte has an address divisible by four. We
should point out that all this is necessary because of hardware requirements. Almost all modern computers are particular about
the alignment of data.

As a COBOL programmer, you do not have to be concerned about the alignment of data if you are defining a binary
(COMP) field. If it should turn out that the binary field does not
have an even-numbered address, the COBOL compiler will arrange things so that (a) the binary field is moved to a properly
aligned area of memory, (b) the specified arithmetic operation is
carried out, and (c) the results are moved back to the original
storage area allocated for the binary field. All of this is transpar-
ent — that is, COBOL makes it look as if the arithmetic operation has taken place directly on the mis-aligned field.

As you might imagine, this moving of binary fields back and forth can be rather time-consuming; in some cases, it can slow your program significantly. We can avoid all of this internal work, however, by adding the clause SYNC to the data definition. SYNC tells the COBOL compiler to leave space, if necessary, between one data field and another — to ensure that each data field begins on the proper boundary. SYNC is an abbreviation for SYNCHRONIZED; either word is acceptable to COBOL. An example of a data item defined with SYNC follows:

05   TABLE-SUB   PIC S99   USAGE IS COMP SYNC   VALUE IS +01.

SYNC ensures that the original definition of TABLE-SUB is properly aligned. Wherever you define a binary field, it is best to include the SYNC clause.

SYNC is used to properly justify a field within *internal* storage; it should not be confused with the JUSTIFIED clause in a data definition. JUSTIFIED is used when moving alphanumeric fields. Why do we need the JUSTIFIED clause? To deal with situations in which we do not want to accept COBOL's normal tendency to left-justify alphanumeric fields. Normally, if a sending alphanumeric field is larger than the receiving field, the extra positions on the right are truncated. For example:

FIELD A   moved to   FIELD B

|BETSY ROSS| |BETSY RO|

Similarly, if the sending field is shorter than the receiving field, the receiving field is left-aligned and blank-filled on the right. To illustrate:

FIELD A   moved to   FIELD B

|BETSY ROSS| |BETSY ROSSbbb|

When we add the JUSTIFIED clause — which can be abbreviated as JUST — to the data definition of the receiving field, the alphanumeric field is right-aligned; and if the receiving field is too short, the extra left-most positions are truncated:

FIELD A   moved to   FIELD B

BETSY ROSS   TSY ROSS

If, on the other hand, the receiving field is longer than the sending field, the field is right-aligned and blank-filled on the left. For example:

FIELD A   moved to   FIELD B

BETSY ROSS   bbbBETSY ROSS

To define a field as JUSTIFIED, we simply code

05   FIELD-B   PIC X(13) JUST.

Remember: The JUSTIFIED clause may be used for elementary alphanumeric items only.

10.4 Negative numbers and the SIGN clause

We have seen that when defining signed numeric fields, it is as easy to define negative numbers as it is to define positive numbers. For example, we can code

01 DISCOUNT   PIC S9V99   COMP-3   VALUE -2.55.

From our discussion in Section 10.2, we know that DISCOUNT would have the following format in internal storage:

255D

In many accounting applications, data is entered with a separate "+" or "−" to represent either a credit or a debit. For example, suppose we are required to write a program to update a sequential master account file, using transaction cards which contain an account number and a numeric quantity with a trailing "+" or "−" representing a credit or debit. Once the matching account is found, we are to adjust the field named ACCOUNT-BALANCE. We could define the card format as follows:

```
01 TRANSACTION-CARD.
     05  ACCOUNT-NUMBER          PIC  9(5).
     05  CARD-AMOUNT             PIC  9(3)V99.
     05  CREDIT-DEBIT            PIC  X.
     05  FILLER                  PIC  X(69).
```

We could then write the following code:

```
IF CREDIT-DEBIT = CREDIT-MARK
    ADD CARD-AMOUNT TO ACCOUNT-BALANCE
ELSE IF CREDIT-DEBIT = DEBIT-MARK
    SUBTRACT CARD-AMOUNT FROM ACCOUNT-BALANCE
ELSE
    PERFORM ERROR-ROUTINE.
```

With this example, CREDIT-MARK is defined as a "+", and DEBIT-MARK is defined as a "−". A positive ACCOUNT-BALANCE would mean a credit, and a negative ACCOUNT-BALANCE would indicate an amount owed by the customer.

There is nothing wrong with the code above − but COBOL allows it to be written much more compactly. We can define the field known as CREDIT-DEBIT as nothing more than the sign for CARD-AMOUNT. This would be done as follows:

```
01 TRANSACTION-CARD.
     05  ACCOUNT-NUMBER      PIC  9(5).
     05  CARD-AMOUNT         PIC  S9(3)V99
             SIGN IS TRAILING SEPARATE CHARACTER.
     05  FILLER              PIC  X(69).
```

We could then write the following code:

    ADD CARD-AMOUNT TO ACCOUNT-BALANCE.
    __*IF CARD-AMOUNT IS NEGATIVE, IT IS A DEBIT.__
    __*IF CARD-AMOUNT IS POSITIVE, IT IS A CREDIT.__

With the SIGN IS TRAILING SEPARATE CHARACTER clause, COBOL counts the "s" in the definition of CARD-AMOUNT as a position. Exactly *where* the S is placed is unimportant — the SIGN clause states that the S is the last character. Without the SIGN IS TRAILING SEPARATE CHARACTER clause, CARD-AMOUNT would be considered to be a five-position field with the sign contained *within* the right-most digit. When the clause is present in your data definition, COBOL considers the field to be a six-position numeric field with the sign *alone* in the right-most position. The SIGN IS . . . clause is permitted only for numeric items with a DISPLAY format. The sign must be either a plus or a minus. If we wanted the sign to immediately *precede* the numeric field, we could have used SIGN IS LEADING SEPARATE CHARACTER.

When we input data from cards, the sign of an amount field can be overpunched on the right-most digit. For example, if a number is to represent a credit, no overpunch is made; thus, an amount of 15075 would simply be keypunched as 15075. However, if the amount is a debit — i.e., a negative quantity — the last digit is overpunched: First, the numeric digit is punched, and then the "−" character is punched over it. Thus, to represent −15075, we would keypunch 15075̄.

How on earth can our COBOL program unravel all of this? It all works because of the EBCDIC coding scheme for numbers and letters. When you punch a "−" character on a standard keypunch, it causes a hole to be placed in the 11-row of the card. Punching a numeric digit, on the other hand, causes a single hole to be punched in any of the 0 through 9 rows. Thus, punching a 5, and then overpunching a "−", causes a hole to be punched in the 5-row of the card, and then another hole to be punched in the 11-row.

This particular combination of punches is equivalent to the alphabetic character N in the EBCDIC coding scheme (you might want to try all of this on your keypunch just to convince yourself). If you look at the EBCDIC table presented in Section 10.2, you'll find that the character N is represented *internally* by the binary sequence 11010101, or the hexadecimal value D5. Which leads us to the point of all this: A hexadecimal D5 can be interpreted as a −5 when that byte is described as S9 in a PICTURE clause. And since the sign of a DISPLAY numeric field is in the zone bits of the low-order digit, 15075 equals -150.75 when the field is described as S9(3)V99.

In situations where we want to explicitly indicate that a number is positive, we can overpunch — but not with a "+", as you might have thought. Because of the coding scheme on the cards, the appropriate character for overpunching a "+" number is the ampersand character, "&".

On many computers, we can overpunch either the right-most digit, *or* the left-most digit. If we overpunch the right-most digit, we use SIGN IS TRAILING SEPARATE CHARACTER, and if we overpunch the left-most digit, we use SIGN IS LEADING SEPARATE CHARACTER. Check the details of your COBOL compiler as well as the standards in your programming group, before you begin using the overpunch facility.

10.5 Editing fields with PIC

When we are asked to write a program that will print some numbers for a report, we are usually expected to print the numbers in their most readable form. For example, a field named NUMBER-OF-CARDS, defined as 9(6), might produce a number like 000024 or 384601 when moved directly to a print-line. However, the program user might prefer seeing just 24; and for large numbers, he might prefer something like 384,601.

How can we ensure that numbers are printed in their most readable form? Well, we could use INSPECT or EXAMINE to replace leading zeroes with spaces. And we could use TALLY to count the number of digits being printed; if the TALLY is greater than three, we could insert a comma by moving the number, one part at a time, to the print-line. However, there is an easier way of doing it. We could simply write the statement

MOVE NUMBER-OF-CARDS TO CARD-TOTAL-ON-LINE.

This is not a feat of prestidigitation, but just an example of editing a field by using the COBOL editing features. The receiving field — the field that receives the number when the MOVE is done — is CARD-TOTAL-ON-LINE. It is defined as follows:

```
01  PRINT-LINE.
    05  CARD-TOTAL-ON-LINE    PIC  ZZZ,ZZZ.
```

The letter Z is a position in the receiving field that automatically causes a leading zero in that position to be converted to a blank. The comma in the PIC clause tells COBOL to insert a comma if a non-blank character precedes it. Here are some more examples of editing specifications in the PIC clause:

PIC & VALUE OF SENDING FIELD		PIC OF RECEIVING FIELD	RESULT
9(5)	01000	ZZ,ZZZ	1,000
9(5)	00227	ZZ,ZZZ	227
9(5)	00000	ZZ,ZZZ	
9(5)	37624	ZZ,ZZZ	37,624

Notice the third example: The result column is blank. Chances are that if you read a report, and saw a line that read NUMBER OF NEW CUSTOMERS ADDED-, you might think that the computer program had an error in it. In a case like this, it would be better to print NUMBER OF NEW CUSTOMERS ADDED - 0.

We can accomplish this by changing the PIC clause of the receiving field to ZZ,ZZ9. The 9 indicates to COBOL that it should print this digit and all subsequent digits, if any — even if the digit is a leading zero. Here are some examples of the Z specification combined with the 9 specification:

PIC & VALUE OF SENDING FIELD		PIC OF RECEIVING FIELD	RESULT
9(5)	12345	Z9,999	12,345
9(5)	00024	Z9,999	0,024
9(5)	00006	ZZ,999	006

We can use a decimal point in the PIC clause in much the same way that we have been using the comma. However, the decimal point does have one special effect: It causes the decimal point of the sending field to be lined up with the decimal point of the receiving field's editing PIC. (By the way, only one decimal point is allowed in each field.) As an example, suppose we have to edit the following field:

05   AVERAGE-ACREAGE-PER-SALE   PIC 9V99.

Now suppose that the receiving field is defined as

05   AVERAGE-ACREAGE-PRINT   PIC 99.999.

Now, if we simply execute the statement

**MOVE AVERAGE-ACREAGE-PER-SALE TO
AVERAGE-ACREAGE-PRINT.**

the fields will be aligned properly. For example, if the sending field had contained the value 4.36, then the result, after moving, would be 04.360. On the other hand, if the editing PIC in the receiving field had been ZZ.99, the result would have been 4.36.

Here are some more examples:

PIC & VALUE OF SENDING FIELD	PIC OF RECEIVING FIELD	RESULT
9(5)V99 01244.68	ZZ,ZZ9.99	1,244.68
9(5)V99 00000.03	ZZ,ZZ9.99	0.03
9(5)V99 00000.03	ZZ,ZZZ.99	.03

Note that the third example resulted in a receiving field of .03 because, unlike the comma, the decimal point in a PIC editing clause terminates any further zero suppression. One last point about commas and decimal points as editing characters: It is illegal for either a decimal point or a comma to be the *last* character in an editing PIC, or for a Z to follow a 9 or a decimal point.

Thus far, we have been illustrating the editing of *unsigned* numeric fields. Now suppose that we are required to show — perhaps on an output report — whether a numeric field is positive or negative. There are several easy ways to do this. Let's take the straightforward case first. If a field is negative, we wish to print a leading "−"; if it is positive, we wish to print the number only. To do this, we use the character "−" in the editing PIC of the receiving field. Remember that the sign is carried in the zone bits of the low-order byte for a DISPLAY format numeric field. In the examples below, we will show the sign of a number above the low-order digit.

PIC & VALUE OF SENDING FIELD	PIC OF RECEIVING FIELD	RESULT
S9(4) 0123̄	-9999	-0123
S9(4) 1234̇	-9999	1234
S9(4) 2468̄	9999-	2468-
S9(4) 3579̇	9999-	3579
S9(4) 0000̄	-9999	0000

Notice that 0000, whether positive or negative, will have a result with no sign. We can suppress leading zeroes and place a minus sign immediately before the first non-zero digit by using the

CHAPTER 10: INTERNAL CODING AND THE DATA DIVISION   95

"—" in the same way we used the Z editing character. The examples below illustrate this.

PIC & VALUE OF SENDING FIELD		PIC OF RECEIVING FIELD	RESULT
S9(4)	0076̄	----9	-76
S9(4)	0076̟̇	----9	76
S9(4)	6666̄	-----	-6666
S9(4)	0000̟̇	----	

When we use zero suppression with the "—" character, we must construct the receiving field with an extra position. If the sending field, for example, has a length of three, then the receiving field must be at least four positions — to accommodate the possible three numeric positions as well as the minus sign.

Now let's imagine that we want to indicate positive numbers by preceding such numbers with a "+" character; at the same time, we want to continue editing negative numbers with a "—" character. All of this can be done with the "+" character in the editing PIC. We can also use the "+" to suppress leading zeroes. Just like the "—", the resulting "+" character can be made to either precede or trail the number. Try to determine the result of each MOVE operation in the exercises below. The answers can be found in the Appendix.

PIC & VALUE OF SENDING FIELD		PIC OF RECEIVING FIELD	RESULT
S9(3)V9	024.6̟̇	+++9.9	
S9(3)V9	006.7̄	+++9.9	
S9(4)	2468̟̇	++,++9	
S9(4)	0022̟̇	++,++9	
S9(3)	001̟̇	+ZZ9	
S9(3)	006̄	+ZZ9	
S9(4)	0016̟̇	ZZZ9-	
S9(2)V99	22.06̄	ZZ.999-	
S9(2)V99	00.01̄	ZZ.99+	

There will be many programming situations in which we know that the numeric quantities represent dollars and cents. Regardless of whether our program produces paychecks, sales reports, or expenditure reports, it usually is desirable to show amounts of money in their most readable form. COBOL supplies an editing PIC with some characters specifically dealing with monetary amounts; as you might expect, the editing character that we use is the dollar sign. We can use "$" to specify either a fixed-position dollar sign, or a floating-position dollar sign. Here are some examples of both:

PIC & VALUE OF SENDING FIELD		PIC OF RECEIVING FIELD	RESULT
9(4)	0022	$ZZZ9	$ 22
9(4)	0022	$$$$9	$22
9(6)	012448	$$$$,$$9	$12,448

When we are dealing with both dollars and cents, we can use the decimal point as well as the "$" in our editing PIC. Once again, this can be done in either a fixed-position format or in a floating-position format. Here are some examples:

PIC & VALUE OF SENDING FIELD		PIC OF RECEIVING FIELD	RESULT
9(3)V99	009.79	$ZZ9.99	$ 9.79
9(3)V99	000.39	$ZZZ.99	$ .39
9(5)V99	06224.71	$$$,$$9.99	$6,224.71
9(5)V99	00016.23	$$$,$$9.99	$16.23

If we have to contend with both negative and positive dollar amounts — e.g., if we are dealing with both credits and debits — then we can use the "+" and "−" editing characters to our advantage. For instance, look at the following editing examples:

PIC & VALUE OF SENDING FIELD	PIC OF RECEIVING FIELD	RESULT
S9(3)V99 022.6$\overline{7}$	$$$9.99-	$22.67-
S9(3)V99 106.0$\overset{+}{2}$	$$$9.99+	$106.02+
S9(3)V99 321.9$\overline{6}$	$$$9.99+	$321.96-
S9(3)V99 016.3$\overset{+}{2}$	$$$9.99-	$16.32

There is another convenient way of dealing with positive and negative dollar amounts. We can print the characters CR (for credit) or DB (for debit) as the right-most characters of the result. It works like this: If a field is negative, then either CR or DB will be printed to the right of the number — depending on which one we specify in the editing PIC. If the field is positive or unsigned, then two spaces will be printed to the right of the number if we have used *either* CR or DB in the editing PIC. Depending on the nature of the application, the person reading our output will have to know whether a negative amount represents a debit or a credit. Here are some examples:

PIC & VALUE OF SENDING FIELD	PIC OF RECEIVING FIELD	RESULT
S99V99 21.4$\overline{3}$	$$9.99CR	$21.43CR
S99V99 00.4$\overset{+}{3}$	$$9.99CR	$0.43
S99V99 62.1$\overline{9}$	$$9.99DB	$62.19DB
99V99 06.77	$$9.99DB	$6.77

Unfortunately, the editing PIC does not give us the facility to print CR for positive numbers and DB for negative numbers — or vice versa. It prints two spaces for positive (or unsigned) numbers, leaving you to determine whether negative numbers should be printed as a CR or a DB. If you do want to print CR next to positive numbers, and DB next to negative numbers, you'll have to do some extra programming of your own.

We have seen that the editing character Z is useful for suppressing leading zeroes and replacing them with blanks. There are some applications in which it may be convenient to re-place leading zeroes by asterisks as follows:

PIC & VALUE OF SENDING FIELD	PIC OF RECEIVING FIELD	RESULT
9(3)V99 004.46	$**9.99	$**4.46

This facility is particularly useful when printing dollar amounts on checks or other financial documents. By filling the area to the left of the high-order digit with asterisks, we make it more difficult for someone to alter the check.

So far, our discussion about editing PIC characters has been confined to numeric fields. Most of the real-world editing prob-lems that you'll face will involve the formatting of numeric quantities on output reports. However, there are also a number of other editing characters that we can use to edit alphanumeric and numeric fields. We can easily instruct COBOL to insert zeroes, blanks, or slashes ("/") in such fields. For example:

PIC & VALUE OF SENDING FIELD		PIC OF RECEIVING FIELD	RESULT
S9(3)	012	$$9.00	$12.00
S9(4)	1446	Z,ZZ9,000	1,446,000
X(6)	XYZ446	XXXBBXXX	XYZ 446
9(10)	2127302670	999/999/9999	212/730/2670
9(9)	085423174	999B99B9999	085 42 3174

As you can see from these examples, simple insertions are useful for formatting Social Security numbers, telephone numbers, and various other fields that are to be stored in a compressed format but printed in a "humanized" format.

We have seen many editing features in this section. Don't be concerned about memorizing them. Whenever you need to print numeric or alphanumeric information in a formatted manner, just consult your COBOL manual to see if one of the PIC editing characters will do the job for you automatically. Certain common editing applications — such as zero suppression — eventually will become so familiar that you won't have to look them up every time you use them.

Before we consider other topics, there are a few final rules about editing — rules that pertain to all of the editing characters we have seen in this section:

1. Once a field has been edited, the edited (receiving) field is considered to be alphanumeric — regardless of whether the sending field was numeric or alphanumeric. After the field has been edited, it can be MOVEd, but *no arithmetic operation can be done with it.*

2. The PIC string for editing may not exceed 30 characters in length, and the receiving field must be long enough to hold the largest possible value of the sending field.

3. Only elementary items may be edited using the editing PIC characters.

10.6 Figurative constants

COBOL has certain reserved words that identify specific constant values. These reserved words are known as *figurative constants*. We already have used two of the most popular figurative constants: SPACES and ZEROES. When comparing a field with either of these constants, the COBOL compiler automatically adjusts the constant to be the same length as that of the other field, so that the comparison will test the entire field. When SPACES or ZEROES are used without reference to a specific field — e.g., in the STRING or UNSTRING statements — the length of the figurative constant is assumed to be one.

The figurative constants HIGH-VALUES and LOW-VALUES are used most often in comparing numeric quantities; as a pair, they are used for testing end-of-file conditions on sequentially ordered files. As you would expect, they are the largest possible number and the smallest possible number that can be represented on the computer. Depending on the specific COBOL compiler, HIGH-VALUES may be represented by a field of all 9's, or it may be represented by a field with hexadecimal FF in every byte. Similarly, LOW-VALUES may be represented by all zeroes, or by hexadecimal 00 in every byte.

Before you use HIGH-VALUES or LOW-VALUES in a programming application, check your COBOL manual to see how they actually are represented internally. This may help you to avoid some subtle, but very unpleasant, bugs in your program. If you find, for example, that HIGH-VALUES is represented internally by a field of all 9's, it may be dangerous to use the field in certain kinds of comparisons. For example, you may be reading records from a master file whose records are in ascending order by customer account number. To determine whether you have reached the end of the file, you might be tempted to code as shown on the following page, but this might cause serious trouble. There could well be a *legitimate* account number whose value is 9999. Indeed, many organizations use an account number (or an employee number, or a part number, or any other kind of number) of all 9's to indicate a special account.

```
        PERFORM READ-MASTER.
        PERFORM PROCESS-MASTER-LOOP
            UNTIL ACCOUNT-NUMBER EQUALS HIGH-VALUES.
        STOP RUN.
        ----------.
        ----------.
        ----------.
    READ-MASTER.
        READ MASTER-FILE
            AT END
                MOVE HIGH-VALUES TO ACCOUNT-NUMBER.
```

Another problem with some compilers is that HIGH- and LOW-VALUES are non-numeric values, that is, X'FF' and X'00', respectively; and may cause compiler diagnostics if they are compared to numeric fields.

A less commonly used figurative constant is QUOTES, having the value of a literal *single* quote, or "'". The QUOTES constant is useful for enclosing a field in quotes on a print-line. Since most such applications require the printing of a *double* quote, we would have to move QUOTES to *two* one-position fields immediately preceding the field we wish to print, and to *two* one-position fields immediately following it.

As we observed earlier, COBOL allows us to spell the figurative constants in a variety of ways. Any of thc following spellings is legal:

SPACE	ZERO	HIGH-VALUE	LOW-VALUE	QUOTE
SPACES	ZEROS	HIGH-VALUES	LOW-VALUES	QUOTES
	ZEROES			

10.7 The RENAMES clause

When defining data, we may need to refer to the same field in several different ways. See, for example, the definition of an employee record on the following page.

```
01  EMPLOYEE-REC.
    05  EMPLOYEE-NUM.
        10  EMPLOYEE-PREFIX        PIC 9(4).
        10  EMPLOYEE-JOB-CODE      PIC 9(2).
    05  EMPLOYEE-NAME              PIC X(30).
    05  DATE-HIRED.
        10  YEAR-HIRED             PIC 9(2).
        10  MONTH-HIRED            PIC 9(2).
        10  DAY-HIRED              PIC 9(2).
    05  FILLER                     PIC X(38).
66  JOB-NAME-FIRST-YEAR
    RENAMES EMPLOYEE-JOB-CODE THRU YEAR-HIRED.
```

With this definition, we can refer to each field defined in the record, and we can separately refer to JOB-NAME-FIRST-YEAR, which includes EMPLOYEE-JOB-CODE, EMPLOYEE-NAME, and YEAR-HIRED. When we use the level-66 RENAMES clause, the RENAMES must *immediately* follow the record that holds the renamed data. It is perfectly legal to use several level-66's to rename the same record, and the data they rename may overlap. For example, we could add another level-66 to the employee record we coded above:

```
66  EMPLOYEE-NUM-AND-NAME
    RENAMES EMPLOYEE-NUM THRU EMPLOYEE-NAME.
```

A RENAMES clause can begin and/or end with a group name. If it does, the span of renamed data begins with the first elementary item of the first group item, and ends with the last elementary item in the last group name.

Although the RENAMES clause can be very handy in some applications, in practice it is seldom used. Indeed, some programming organizations do not permit the use of RENAMES. Such organizations argue that the use of RENAMES could cause problems if the record definition changes. For example, if a new field is inserted in the middle of a record, it may affect the span of a RENAMES.

10.8 The REDEFINES clause

In COBOL applications, it is very common to read a file that contains different kinds of records. For example, we may be reading a card file that contains an information card and an account card for each customer. To handle a case like this, we would probably code two 01-level record descriptions, with the FD for the card file. Within the FD statement, we would expect to see the clause

DATA RECORDS ARE CUSTOMER-INFO
ACCOUNT-INFO.

What have we done? First, we have defined the records in the card file as CUSTOMER-INFO; then, we have *redefined* the same area in storage, and told COBOL that the specified area will contain records known as ACCOUNT-INFO. The redefinition of the record area is accomplished by listing all the 01-level records in the DATA RECORDS ARE . . . clause.

While this approach is appropriate for the redefinition of entire records, it is not sufficient when we want to redefine a portion of a record, or certain WORKING-STORAGE fields. To accomplish this, we use the REDEFINES clause, as demonstrated by the following example:

```
05  CURRENCY-CODE                    PIC X.
    88  U-S-A                         VALUE 'U'.
    88  JAPAN                         VALUE 'J'.
    88  FRANCE                        VALUE 'F'.
05  DOLLARS-CENTS                     PIC 9(4)V99.
05  YEN REDEFINES DOLLARS-CENTS PIC 9(6).
05  FRANCS-CENTIMES REDEFINES
        DOLLARS-CENTS                 PIC 9(4)V99.
```

The storage area is shown on the next page:

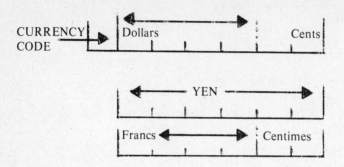

We could now code:

```
IF U-S-A
     MOVE DOLLARS-CENTS TO AMT-DUE
ELSE IF JAPAN
     MULTIPLY YEN BY JAPAN-RATE GIVING AMT-DUE
ELSE IF FRANCE
     MULTIPLY FRANCS-CENTIMES BY FRANCE-RATE
          GIVING AMT-DUE
ELSE
     PERFORM ERROR-ROUTINE.
```

We can use REDEFINES to redefine either a group item or an elementary item. However, in all cases, the level given to the description of the redefinition must be the same as that of the original definition; also, the REDEFINES statement must immediately follow the field being redefined. Redefinition concludes when a level-number equal to or less than the redefinition level is encountered. To illustrate this, here's an example of an illegal REDEFINES:

```
05  A.
     10  B            PIC X(2).
     10  C            PIC X(4).
05  Q REDEFINES B     PIC 9(2).
```

This is illegal because the REDEFINES statement is at an 05-level, and it is attempting to redefine a field of data that was defined as a 10-level. To do it correctly, we would code as follows:

```
05  A.
    10  B                    PIC X(2).
    10  Q REDEFINES B        PIC 9(2).
    10  C                    PIC X(4).
```

Here's an example of a legal redefinition of a data item:

```
05  A.
    10  B                    PIC X(2).
    10  C                    PIC X(4).
05  Q REDEFINES A.
    10  R                    PIC X.
    10  S.
        15  T                PIC 9(2).
        15  U                PIC X(3).
05  Z.
----------.
----------.
----------.
```

Note that a redefinition of data does not have to involve the same data type as the original definition. For example, the original definition of A above was alphanumeric (as indicated by the definition of the elementary items B and C); but T is defined as numeric. This is perfectly legal.

10.9 Example

To illustrate many of the concepts discussed in this chapter, let's imagine that we have to write a program named FORMATDL. Its job will be to format detail lines for a billing report associated with tour sales of the Wing & Prayer organization, discussed in Chapter 8.

Our program will be CALLed by BILLREPT, and will be given a client record to format. When FORMATDL has properly formatted the line, it should CALL a subordinate module PRINTDL, passing a detail line as its only parameter. Thus, we are dealing with a structure chart that looks like the one on the following page.

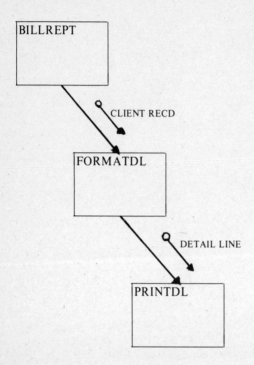

When FORMATDL is called, it is given a fixed length record, CLIENT-RECD, which is 80 positions long, and has the following format:

FIELD	TYPE	POSITIONS
Client Number	Numeric	1-6 (6)
Independent/Agent	Alpha (I or A)	7 (1)
Tour Number	Numeric	8-13 (6)
Client Name	Alphanumeric	14-43 (30)
Number in Group	Numeric	44-45 (2)
Cost for One	Signed Numeric ($$$$¢¢)	46-51 (6)
Deposit	Signed Numeric ($$$$¢¢)	52-59 (8)
Departure Date	Numeric (YYMMDD)	60-65 (6)
Filler	–	66-80 (15)

The output print-line is 132 positions long. It is to be formatted in slightly different ways, depending on whether the client is an independent or a travel agent:

POSITIONS	FIELD	FORMAT
1-5	Filler	Spaces
6-13	Tour Number	99/999/9
14-18	Filler	Spaces
19-25	Client Number	9/99999 (if independent)
26	Filler	Space (if independent)
19-26	Client Number	99/999/9 (if agent)
27-31	Filler	Spaces
32-61	Client Name	30 Alphanumeric positions
62-66	Filler	Spaces
67-68	Number in Group	99 − suppress leading zeroes
69-73	Filler	Spaces
74-84	Total Cost	$999,999.99 − float $, suppress leading zeroes
85-89	Filler	Spaces
90-100	Deposit	$999,999.99 − float $, suppress leading zeroes
101-105	Filler	Spaces
106-119	Balance Due	$999,999.99CR − float $, suppress leading zeroes
120-124	Filler	Spaces
125-132	Departure Date	MM/DD/YY

The Total Cost field is computed as the Cost for One multiplied by the Number in Group. Similarly, the Balance Due field is computed as Total Cost minus Deposit. If the Deposit is larger than the Total Cost, then CR should appear following the Balance Due.

When the output line is properly formatted, we should CALL PRINTDL, and pass the line as a parameter.

Take some time to study these specifications, and then try writing the program. Do *not* look at the sample program in the Appendix until you've made an attempt of your own.

11 Using Tables

11.1 Introduction

In this chapter, we discuss one of the most important concepts in programming: tables. Programmers often talk about tables, arrays, subscripts, pointers, and indexes when they discuss their programming applications; indeed, you will sometimes hear programmers discuss an approach to programming known as *table-driven programs.*

The first objective of this chapter is to make you aware of the usefulness and importance of this table-oriented approach to programming. Then, we will discuss the method of defining tables in the COBOL DATA DIVISION as well as the methods of accessing tables in the PROCEDURE DIVISION.

Surprisingly, many veteran COBOL programmers are not familiar (or comfortable) with the concept of tables. In our opinion, skill at table-handling is one of the things that distinguishes a good COBOL programmer from an average one. So, we urge you to read this chapter carefully and practice the examples — it will pay off!

11.2 Defining related data items

Let's imagine that we want to write a program that totals our company's sales on a product-by-product basis. The company sells 25 different products, each with its own unique product code. A clever systems analyst has assigned unique codes of 01 through 25 to the products.

Obviously, we need 25 accumulators to hold the daily sales totals for each product. We could define the accumulators in WORKING-STORAGE as follows:

```
01   PRODUCT-TOTALS.
     05   ACCUM01      PIC S9(5).
     05   ACCUM02      PIC S9(5).
     05   ACCUM03      PIC S9(5).
     ----------.
     ----------.
     ----------.
     05   ACCUM25      PIC S9(5).
```

Let's assume that the details of each sale of a specific product are keypunched on a card, defined in WORKING-STORAGE as follows:

```
01   SALE.
     05   PRODUCT-CODE PIC 99.
     05   NUMBER-SOLD   PIC 9(3).
```

In order to accumulate the sales of each product properly, we could write the following code in the PROCEDURE DIVISION:

```
IF PRODUCT-CODE = '01'
   ADD NUMBER-SOLD TO ACCUM01
ELSE IF PRODUCT-CODE = '02'
   ADD NUMBER-SOLD TO ACCUM02
ELSE IF . . .
   ----------.
   ----------.
   ----------.
ELSE IF PRODUCT-CODE = '25'
   ADD NUMBER-SOLD TO ACCUM25.
```

Although this approach will solve the problem, it is time-consuming, error-prone, and boring. And what if the company has 2,500 products instead of just 25?

Fortunately, COBOL enables us to handle problems of this type much more easily. Instead of defining each of the 25 accumulators separately, we can write

```
01   PRODUCT-TOTALS.
     05   ACCUM      PIC S9(5)    OCCURS 25 TIMES.
```

By using the OCCURS clause, space is reserved for 25 S9(5) fields, just as if we had defined each one individually. In this fashion, we have created a table of accumulators — a table whose entries all are named ACCUM. However, we no longer have a unique name for each of the 25 fields — for example, there is no longer an ACCUM17 to which we can refer.

Obviously, we must have some way to add the NUMBER-SOLD into the proper accumulator. How can we do this? By using the PRODUCT-CODE field as the key to the proper accumulator for the addition of NUMBER-SOLD. The definitions of PRODUCT-CODE and NUMBER-SOLD remain the same:

```
01   SALE.
     05   PRODUCT-CODE      PIC 99.
     05   NUMBER-SOLD       PIC 9(3).
```

Since PRODUCT-CODE is the key to the proper accumulator, it can be used as a subscript, or "pointer," for ACCUM; that is, it acts as a pointer to the particular occurrence of ACCUM that is to be used. We make use of this concept by writing the following statement in the PROCEDURE DIVISION:

ADD NUMBER-SOLD TO ACCUM (PRODUCT-CODE).

When we use a field as a pointer to a specific item of data within an OCCURS clause, the pointer field is known as a subscript; PRODUCT-CODE is a subscript in the example above.

When a field is used as a subscript, it must be enclosed in parentheses. Most COBOL compilers are very finicky about one other formatting aspect of subscripts: There must be *at least* one space between the table name (the field defined within an OCCURS clause) and the opening parenthesis of the subscript. Thus,

ADD NUMBER-SOLD TO ACCUM(PRODUCT-CODE).

is *not* correct COBOL syntax for all compilers, while

ADD NUMBER-SOLD TO ACCUM   (PRODUCT-CODE).

is correct on all compilers.

One other point: Any field may be used as a subscript (in addition to being used for other computational purposes) as long as it is defined as one of the numeric types of data.

It should be evident from this simple example that subscripting — and the use of tables — allows us to code many applications much more simply. Keep in mind that the alternative to subscripting would be to write out a long sequence of code in the form

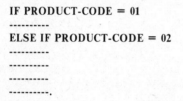

```
IF PRODUCT-CODE = 01
----------
ELSE IF PRODUCT-CODE = 02
----------
----------
----------
----------.
```

Q.   Is there any other way to organize the code for the example discussed above?

A.   Yes. We could use a GO TO DEPENDING ON statement and write the following code:

```
          GO TO P1, P2, . . . , P25
          DEPENDING ON PRODUCT-CODE.
```

Q.   What are the advantages and disadvantages of the three approaches we have seen for implementing the sales-totals application?

A.   The nature of the programming application will usually determine which of the three approaches is most appropriate. If, for example, we had only three product codes in the example above, and if we could be sure that the company would not require new product codes in the future, it probably would be simpler to use the IF . . . ELSE IF . . . coding approach. After all, it doesn't require setting up a table with an OCCURS clause.

The GO TO DEPENDING ON approach has the advantage

(with most implementations of COBOL) of being reasonably efficient. Within the computer hardware, control is transferred to the appropriate paragraph with machine instructions very similar to the subscripting approach that we have already seen in COBOL. However, the GO TO DEPENDING ON approach does have the disadvantage of requiring 25 separate paragraph-names (in the sales-totals example). Thus, while it is fairly efficient in terms of execution speed, this approach usually will be relatively inefficient in terms of memory requirements. The GO TO DEPENDING ON approach is most practical when different types of processing must be carried out for each value of the subscript.

Assuming that there are more than three or four distinct values of the subscript variable and that the processing to be carried out for each distinct variable is virtually the same (e.g., adding NUMBER-SOLD to the appropriate accumulator), the subscript approach is easier to code, more efficient in terms of execution speed and memory requirements, and generally much easier to change.

11.3 Defining tables

As we saw in the example in Section 11.2, identical data items often can be defined with the OCCURS clause. In most instances, this data must be defined internally, in the WORKING-STORAGE SECTION of the program. When data are defined by the programmer in this way, the group of items is called a table.

Let's look at another example to illustrate the use of tables. At the end of Chapter 8, you were asked to design a program to edit incoming transactions for the charter airline booking system. One of the modules in our solution shown in the Appendix is called CHECKAIR. This module's function is to check to see if Airport Choice is valid. CHECKAIR is given a three-position Airport Code and a three-position "valid-invalid" switch. The module's purpose is to set the switch appropriately. While there are many ways of coding CHECKAIR, one easy way is to use a table of valid Airport Codes. We might write the following:

```
IDENTIFICATION DIVISION.
PROGRAM-ID. CHECKAIR.

ENVIRONMENT DIVISION.

DATA DIVISION.

WORKING-STORAGE SECTION.
01   AIRPORT-ABBREVIATIONS.
     05   FILLER                 PIC X(3)    VALUE 'JFK'.
     05   FILLER                 PIC X(3)    VALUE 'LAX'.
     05   FILLER                 PIC X(3)    VALUE 'SFO'.
     05   FILLER                 PIC X(3)    VALUE 'ORD'.
     05   FILLER                 PIC X(3)    VALUE 'DFW'.
     05   FILLER                 PIC X(3)    VALUE 'IAD'.
01   AIRPORT-TABLE REDEFINES AIRPORT-ABBREVIATIONS.
     05   AIRPORT
              OCCURS 6 TIMES     PIC X(3).
01   THIS-AIRPORT               PIC S9(8)    COMP SYNC.
01   NUMBER-OF-AIRPORTS         PIC S9(3)    COMP-3    VALUE 6.

LINKAGE SECTION.
01   AIRPORT-CODE               PIC X(3).
01   FOUND-AIR-SW               PIC X(3).
   .
   .
   .

PROCEDURE DIVISION
     USING       AIRPORT-CODE
                 FOUND-AIR-SW.
LOOKUP-AIR.
     MOVE 'NO ' TO FOUND-AIR-SW.
     MOVE 1 TO THIS-AIRPORT.
     PERFORM CHECK-AIR
         UNTIL FOUND-AIR-SW = 'YES'
             OR THIS-AIRPORT IS GREATER THAN
                 NUMBER-OF-AIRPORTS.
EXIT-CHECKAIR.
     EXIT PROGRAM.
CHECK-AIR.
     IF AIRPORT-CODE = AIRPORT (THIS-AIRPORT)
         MOVE 'YES' TO FOUND-AIR-SW
     ELSE
         ADD 1 TO THIS-AIRPORT.
```

Note that the AIRPORT-TABLE shown on the previous page is defined slightly differently from the ACCUM example in Section 11.2. In this program, we not only have to reserve enough space for the definition of the six airports (six fields of PIC X(3)), but we also have to define their values: JFK, LAX, SFO, ORD, DFW, and IAD. Having defined the data, we REDEFINE the same area as six identical occurrences of one field named AIRPORT.

We also have to define a field that will be used as the subscript of the table. In this example, the subscript has been named THIS-AIRPORT. Incidentally, note that we defined THIS-AIRPORT as S9(8) COMP SYNC. That's because the IBM COBOL compiler will automatically convert any subscript to this form if it's not already defined that way. By defining THIS-AIRPORT as S9(8) COMP SYNC, we avoid a lot of inefficient internal conversions of THIS-AIRPORT while the program is running.

Not only do tables permit us to code simply, but they also make maintenance much easier. For example, what if we decide that our charter business should handle flights from St. Louis? Since the Airport Code is STL, we add one entry to AIRPORTS

```
05   FILLER      PIC X(3)   VALUE 'STL'.
```

We would then change the OCCURS clause in AIRPORT-TABLE from 6 to 7, and change the VALUE clause in NUMBER-OF-AIRPORTS from 6 to 7. Without even touching the PROCEDURE DIVISION, the change is complete.

Now let's make the problem a little more difficult. Imagine that CHECKAIR is to return the full name of the city if the Airport Code is valid. To make this work, the module that calls CHECKAIR will have to pass a third parameter: a 15-position field called CITY, which will receive the full name of the city. The code for this enhanced version of CHECKAIR follows:

```
IDENTIFICATION DIVISION.
PROGRAM-ID. CHECKAIR.
ENVIRONMENT DIVISION.
DATA DIVISION.
WORKING-STORAGE SECTION.
01    AIRPORT-ABBREVIATIONS.
      05   ENTRY-1.
           10   FILLER              PIC X(3)        VALUE 'JFK'.
           10   FILLER              PIC X(15)       VALUE 'NEW YORK'.
      05   ENTRY-2.
           10   FILLER              PIC X(3)        VALUE 'LAX'.
           10   FILLER              PIC X(15)       VALUE 'LOS ANGELES'.
      05   ENTRY-3.
           10   FILLER              PIC X(3)        VALUE 'SFO'.
           10   FILLER              PIC X(15)       VALUE 'SAN FRANCISCO'.
      05   ENTRY-4.
           10   FILLER              PIC X(3)        VALUE 'ORD'.
           10   FILLER              PIC X(15)       VALUE 'CHICAGO'.
      05   ENTRY-5.
           10   FILLER              PIC X(3)        VALUE 'DFW'.
           10   FILLER              PIC X(15)       VALUE 'DALLAS-FT WORTH'.
      05   ENTRY-6.
           10   FILLER              PIC X(3)        VALUE 'IAD'.
           10   FILLER              PIC X(15)       VALUE 'WASHINGTON DC'.
01    AIRPORT-TABLE REDEFINES AIRPORT-ABBREVIATIONS.
      05   FILLER
                 OCCURS 6 TIMES.
           10   AIRPORT             PIC X(3).
           10   AIR-CITY            PIC X(15).
01    THIS-AIRPORT                  PIC S9(8)       COMP SYNC.
01    NUMBER-OF-AIRPORTS            PIC S9(3)       COMP-3   VALUE 6.
LINKAGE SECTION.
01    AIRPORT-CODE                  PIC X(3).
01    FOUND-AIR-SW                  PIC X(3).
01    CITY                          PIC X(15).
PROCEDURE DIVISION
      USING      AIRPORT-CODE
                 FOUND-AIR-SW
                 CITY.
LOOKUP-AIR.
      MOVE SPACES TO CITY.
      MOVE 'NO' TO FOUND-AIR-SW.
      MOVE 1 TO THIS-AIRPORT.
      PERFORM CHECK-AIR
          UNTIL FOUND-AIR-SW = 'YES'
              OR THIS-AIRPORT IS GREATER THAN
                  NUMBER-OF-AIRPORTS.
EXIT-CHECKAIR.
      EXIT PROGRAM.
CHECK-AIR.
      IF AIRPORT-CODE = AIRPORT (THIS-AIRPORT)
          MOVE 'YES' TO FOUND-AIR-SW
          MOVE AIR-CITY (THIS-AIRPORT) TO CITY
      ELSE
          ADD 1 TO THIS-AIRPORT.
```

Note that it is perfectly legal, and often very useful, to define a table with more than one field in each entry. Each field within the table can be pointed to by a single subscript.

11.4 Indexes and the SET statement

There is an interesting difference between the subscripting example in Section 11.2 and the airport example in Section 11.3. In Section 11.2, a variable called PRODUCT-CODE was already available for use as a subscript; that is, PRODUCT-CODE would have been a part of the program regardless of whether we had used a table. On the other hand, a field had to be defined for use as a subscript for the table of airports; THIS-AIRPORT had nothing to do with the definition of the problem.

When there is no field that will act naturally as a subscript, it often is preferable to define a field as an *index* instead of as a subscript. The following code redefines the airport table using the INDEXED BY clause:

```
01  AIRPORT-TABLE
        OCCURS 6 TIMES
        INDEXED BY AIRPORT-IND.
    05  AIRPORT-CODE      PIC X(3).
    05  AIRPORT-CITY      PIC X(15).
```

When a field is named with the INDEXED BY clause, we don't have to define it elsewhere. The COBOL compiler internally gives it a PIC clause. One great advantage of indexes is that they are declared within the definition of the table. This usually makes table-related code much easier to follow.

There is a special set of instructions for adjusting the values of an index. Just as with subscripts, it is the programmer's responsibility to initialize and adjust index values. Arithmetic and MOVE statements may not be used with indexes; instead, all indexes are SET, as shown by the following examples:

1. SET AIRPORT-IND TO 1 (to point the index at the first entry in the table)

2. SET AIRPORT-IND TO AIR-CODE (the value of the field AIR-CODE is adjusted to the value of AIRPORT-IND)

3. SET AIRPORT-IND UP BY 1 (add 1 to the existing value of AIRPORT-IND)

4. SET AIRPORT-IND DOWN BY AIR-CODE (subtract the value of AIR-CODE from the value of AIRPORT-IND)

Examples 1 and 2 are functionally equivalent to the MOVE statement. Example 3 is the equivalent of an ADD statement. Example 4 is the index equivalent of a SUBTRACT statement. If you inadvertently attempt to carry out a MOVE statement or arithmetic on an index, the COBOL compiler will issue an error message when it compiles your program.

For practice, recode the last version of CHECKAIR (the one that returns a full city name) using indexes instead of subscripts.

11.5 Sequential searches

For most of the remainder of this chapter, we will be talking about the *searching* techniques of COBOL. Searching means nothing more than looking through items in a table to find a specific item. The most common method of searching is known as a sequential, or linear, search. By sequential, we mean that our program proceeds one entry at a time, starting with the first entry in the table, until the desired entry is found. The searches in our airport examples in the previous sections were sequential in nature.

Let's take a look at another example: Assume that we are given a shuffled deck of cards, and are asked to find the eight of clubs in the deck. Using a sequential search, we would start at the top of the deck — i.e., the first entry — and proceed, card by card, until we find the eight of clubs. We may find our card at the top of the deck, but, if we're unlucky, it may be the last card that we draw. On average, given absolutely random shuffling of the deck, we would expect to find the eight of clubs in 26 examinations.

In a COBOL program, the sequential search is accomplished by initializing a subscript or index to the value one — thereby pointing to the first entry in the table. A PERFORM UNTIL loop is then implemented, with the loop terminated when the search is complete, or when the end of the table is reached. As seen in the airport examples, the paragraph that is invoked by the PERFORM UNTIL must increment the pointer by using an ADD or a SET.

The following pseudocode summarizes this:

```
initialize subscript or index to first entry
WHILE the desired entry has not been found
        and there are more entries in the table
    check if this is the desired entry
    IF it is not the desired entry
        increment subscript or index by 1
```

COBOL offers a variation of the PERFORM UNTIL, which will accomplish the initialization of the subscript, the incrementing of the subscript, and the termination of the loop in a single statement. With the addition of the VARYING, FROM, and BY clauses to the PERFORM UNTIL, we accomplish all of the work necessary to step sequentially through a table. Following is an example:

```
                                       ⎰ SUBSCRIPT ⎱
PERFORM TABLE-LOOKUP VARYING  ⎱ INDEX         ⎰
    FROM 1 BY 1
        UNTIL ENTRY (SUB) = desired entry
        OR SUB GREATER THAN number of entries
```

The FROM clause takes care of initialization, allowing the programmer to initialize a subscript or index to any desired value — even the value of another field. In most cases, however, initializing the subscript or index to point to the first entry in the table will be sufficient; the BY clause will handle the increment-ing of the pointer-field. In the example above, the pointer-field is set to the value one the first time the loop is executed; it is then incremented by one for each successive iteration. The VARYING clause names the field that will be initialized by the FROM clause and incremented by the value stated in the BY clause. The UNTIL statement acts exactly as it does in a simple PERFORM-UNTIL. (Remember that if the UNTIL clause is true immediately after initializing the subscript or index, the loop will not be executed at all.)

To obtain some practice in the use of tables and the PER-FORM VARYING statement, try the following: Write a CALLed program that will calculate the amount due on book orders. Eight different books are available to customers, with the cost per book depending on the number of books ordered. Each book has its own code — 01 through 08. Here is a list of the book prices:

Book code	Unit price 1-5 books	Unit price 6-11 books	Unit price 12 or more books
01	9.95	8.95	7.00
02	16.50	14.00	12.00
03	34.49	32.49	28.00
04	7.75	7.25	6.75
05	12.50	11.50	10.50
06	3.50	3.50	3.50
07	19.95	18.50	17.00
08	4.00	3.50	2.95

Give the program a two-position, numeric BOOK-CODE field; in addition, use a two-position, numeric field identifying the number of books ordered, and a six-position — S9(4)V99 — numeric field called AMT-DUE. Your program should calculate the amount due for the order placed, and return the information to the CALLing program in the AMT-DUE field. If the BOOK-CODE field is not 01 through 08, your program should return zeroes in AMT-DUE. Assume that the information in BOOK-CODE will al-ways be numeric, even though it possibly may be out of range.

The solution can be found in the Appendix.

11.6 The SEARCH and SEARCH ALL statements

Instead of using the PERFORM-VARYING-FROM-BY-UNTIL to carry out a table search, you can take advantage of two built-in COBOL statements: SEARCH and SEARCH ALL.

The SEARCH statement is used to carry out *sequential* table searches of the type we saw in Section 11.5 — i.e., a search that proceeds, one entry at a time, through the entire table. The SEARCH statement automatically picks up the index from the name of the table being searched. This means that there must be an INDEXED BY clause with the table definition if we are to use the SEARCH statement. An example of the SEARCH statement follows:

```
* THIS CODE IS BASED ON THE SOLUTION OF
* THE BOOK-CODE PROBLEM AT THE BACK OF THE BOOK

CALC-AMT-DUE.
   SEARCH BOOK-ENTRY
      VARYING THIS-BOOK
      AT END
         MOVE ZEROES TO AMT-DUE
      WHEN BOOK-CODE-TB (THIS-BOOK) = BOOK-CODE-LK
         MOVE 'YES' TO BOOK-FOUND.

   IF BOOK-FOUND NOT EQUAL TO 'YES'

* THE CODE TO FIND THE AMOUNT DUE WOULD BE HERE, NOW
* THAT WE KNOW THE UNIT PRICE OF THE BOOK.
```

Note that the AT END clause will be activated when the end of the table has been reached and no true conditions were found with the WHEN clause. After the AT END clause is invoked, control passes to the first statement following the period in the SEARCH statement.

You can have as many WHEN clauses as you wish in a single SEARCH statement. However, keep in mind that there is an implied OR condition connecting each of the WHEN clauses.

There are times when a sequential search is not the best way of locating an entry in a table; in such cases, we can use the COBOL SEARCH ALL statement to carry out a *binary* search. Instead of starting at the first entry of a table and searching one by one, we begin in the *middle* of the table, and proceed by cutting the table successively in half, then in half again. In order to carry out such a search, the table must be arranged in ascending or descending order on the field that we are using as a search key.

Using our book-code table, we will test to see if the book code in the middle of the table matches the order — i.e., the fourth entry in the table. If so, the search is finished; if not, we can eliminate either the "top" half of the table or the "bottom" half. For example, if the comparison indicates that BOOK-CODE is greater than the fourth entry in the table, we can disregard the first, second, and third entries. Now only 05, 06, 07, and 08 are possible matches. Once again, COBOL tries the entry in the middle.

Since the strategy is based on dividing by two and then comparing, it is called binary. By continuing to narrow the number of possible entries, the SEARCH ALL can discover the match (or the fact that there are *no* matches) in far fewer tries than generally is possible with the sequential search.

For example, let's assume that we have a table with 64 entries. With a sequential search, we can expect an average of 32 comparisons in order to get a match, while a binary search will make six comparisons at most.

The larger the table, the more likely it is that the binary comparison will be preferable to a sequential search. For example, if our table is 32,768 entries long, then a sequential search will require (on average) 16,384 comparisons, while a binary search will require only 15. Remember that the binary search is preferable only if

1.   The table is ordered in a sequence.

2.   Any one entry is as likely to be the matching entry as is any other entry.

The SEARCH ALL statement could be used as follows:

```
* THIS CODE IS ALSO BASED ON THE BOOK-CODE SOLUTION
 .
 .
 .
01  BOOK-TABLE REDEFINES BOOK-VALUES.
    05  BOOK-ENTRY
            OCCURS 8 TIMES
            ASCENDING KEY IS BOOK-CODE-TB
            INDEXED BY THIS-BOOK.
 .
 .
 .

CALC-AMT-DUE.
    SEARCH ALL BOOK-ENTRY
        AT END
            MOVE ZEROES TO AMT-DUE
        WHEN BOOK-CODE-TB (THIS-BOOK) = BOOK-CODE-LK
            MOVE 'YES' TO BOOK-FOUND.

    IF BOOK-FOUND NOT EQUAL TO 'YES'

* THE CODE TO CALCULATE THE AMOUNT-DUE WOULD BE
* HERE, NOW THAT WE KNOW THE UNIT PRICE OF THE BOOK
```

Notice that when we REDEFINE the table, we add the clause ASCENDING KEY IS BOOK-CODE-TB. The SEARCH ALL requires this clause as a source of information about the *order* of the table layout. Where it is appropriate, we can also use the clause DESCENDING KEY IS. . . . However, whether we arrange the table layout in ascending or descending order, the key must be a numeric data type.

11.7 Multidimensional tables

Sometimes, it is useful to have a *multidimensional* table — that is, a table of tables. For example, a two-dimensional table is organized like a simple table — but each entry within the table is, in itself, a table. To properly manipulate such a table, we need two subscripts, or two indexes. One index points to the entries of the outer table; visualize this pointer as operating vertically. The other index points at the specific entries within the outer entry; think of this pointer as moving horizontally.

To illustrate this concept, let's return to the airport problem. Now, instead of confirming that the airport is one that our charter business uses, we must also confirm that the airline is valid for that specific airport. The specifications remain the same as before, except that a new two-dimensional alpha field is now passed; this field is the AIRLINE-CODE. We use up to four different airlines from any given airport. We will arrange a two-dimensional table of airports and their airlines; to manipulate the table, we will need an index to point at the airports, and another index to point at the airlines. The table looks like this:

	Index to slide along airlines			
	JFK	PA	TW	BA	AF
Index	ORD	PA	AF	TW	
to	LAX	QA	PA		
slide	SFO	PA	AJ	TW	
along	DFW	AM	PA		
airports	IAD	AF	TW	PA	BA

PA = Pan American
TW = Trans World Airlines
BA = British Airways
AF = Air France
QA = Qantas Airways
AJ = Air Japan
AM = Aeronaves de Mexico

Now look at our sample code for the expanded airline example:

```
WORKING-STORAGE SECTION.
01   AIR-VALUES.
     05   FILLER                    PIC X(3)  VALUE 'JFK'.
     05   FILLER                    PIC X(8)  VALUE 'PATWBAAF'.
     05   FILLER                    PIC X(3)  VALUE 'ORD'.
     05   FILLER                    PIC X(8)  VALUE 'PAAFTW   '.
     05   FILLER                    PIC X(3)  VALUE 'LAX'.
     05   FILLER                    PIC X(8)  VALUE 'QAPA    '.
     05   FILLER                    PIC X(3)  VALUE 'SFO'.
     05   FILLER                    PIC X(8)  VALUE 'PAAJTW  '.
     05   FILLER                    PIC X(3)  VALUE 'DFW'.
     05   FILLER                    PIC X(8)  VALUE 'AMPA     '.
     05   FILLER                    PIC X(3)  VALUE 'IAD'.
     05   FILLER                    PIC X(8)  VALUE 'AFTWPABA '.
01   AIR-TABLE REDEFINES AIR-VALUES.
     05   AIRPORT-ENTRY
                    OCCURS 6 TIMES
                    INDEXED BY THIS-PORT.
          10   AIRPORT-TB           PIC X(3).
          10   LINE-ENTRY.
               15   AIRLINE-TB      PIC X(2)
                    OCCURS 4 TIMES
                    INDEXED BY THIS-LINE.
01   LINES-PER-PORT                 PIC S9    VALUE 4.
01   NOT-YES-NOT-NO                 PIC X(3)  VALUE 'XXX'.
01   NOT-FOUND                      PIC X(3)  VALUE 'NO '.
01   FOUND                          PIC X(3)  VALUE 'YES'.

LINKAGE SECTION.
01   AIRPORT-LK                     PIC X(3).
01   AIRLINE-LK                     PIC X(2).
01   FOUND-SW-LK                    PIC X(3).


PROCEDURE DIVISION
     USING        AIRPORT-LK
                  AIRLINE-LK
                  FOUND-SW-LK.
CHECK-CARRIERS.
     MOVE NOT-YES-NOT-NO TO FOUND-SW-LK.
     SET THIS-PORT TO 1.
     SEARCH AIRPORT-ENTRY
          VARYING THIS-PORT
          AT END
               MOVE NOT-FOUND TO FOUND-SW-LK
          WHEN AIRPORT-LK = AIRPORT-TB (THIS-PORT)
               PERFORM FIND-LINE
                    VARYING THIS-LINE
                    FROM 1 BY 1
                    UNTIL AIRLINE-TB (THIS-LINE) OF LINE-ENTRY (THIS-PORT) = AIRLINE-LK
                              OR THIS-LINE GREATER THAN LINES-PER-PORT
               IF THIS-LINE GREATER THAN LINES-PER-PORT
                    MOVE NOT-FOUND TO FOUND-SW-LK
               ELSE
                    MOVE FOUND TO FOUND-SW-LK.
CHECK-EXIT.
     EXIT PROGRAM.
FIND-LINE.
     EXIT.
* A DUMMY PARAGRAPH FOR AIRLINE LOOKUP.
```

The reason we use a PERFORM-VARYING-FROM-BY-UNTIL to check the airlines is that COBOL will not permit us to subscript or index the name of the field we SEARCH. That is, we may *not* code SEARCH LINE-ENTRY (THIS-PORT) . . .

11.8 Variable length tables

Sometimes, tables have a variable number of entries; that is, the number of entries varies from one execution of the program to another. We can easily define such tables with the COBOL OCCURS X TO Y DEPENDING ON clause. For example, here is a module that selects records having account numbers corresponding to an entry in a passed table. A table containing the number of entries is also passed to the CALLed program:

```
IDENTIFICATION DIVISION.
PROGRAM-ID. SELECTRD.

ENVIRONMENT DIVISION.

INPUT-OUTPUT SECTION.
FILE CONTROL.
     SELECT SELECT-RECDS
          ASSIGN TO SYS005-UT-2400-S.

DATA DIVISION.

FILE SECTION.
FD   SELECT-RECDS
     LABEL RECORDS ARE OMITTED.
     DATA RECORD IS PICKED-RECD.
01   PICKED-RECD                          PIC X(100).

WORKING-STORAGE SECTION.

LINKAGE SECTION.
01   NUMBER-ENTRIES -                     PIC S9(2).
01   RECD-IN. -
     05   ACCT-NO-RECD                     PIC 9(5).
     05   FILLER                           PIC X(95).
01   ACCT-NO-TABLE.-
     05   ACCT-NO-TB
          OCCURS 1 TO 99 TIMES
          DEPENDING ON NUMBER-ENTRIES
          ASCENDING KEY IS ACCT-ENTRY
          INDEXED BY THIS-ENTRY.
          10   ACCT-ENTRY                  PIC 9(5).

PROCEDURE DIVISION
     USING        NUMBER-ENTRIES
                  RECD-IN
                  ACCT-NO-TABLE.
SELECT-RECD.
     OPEN INPUT SELECT-RECDS.
     SEARCH ALL ACCT-NO-TB
          WHEN ACCT-ENTRY (THIS-ENTRY) = ACCT-NO-RECD
               WRITE PICKED-RECD FROM RECD-IN.
     CLOSE SELECT-RECDS.
SELECT-RECD-EXIT.
     EXIT PROGRAM.
```

Note that the PROCEDURE DIVISION code remains the same for fixed length and variable length tables, since the OCCURS DEPENDING ON clause lets us hide the variations from the code.

11.9 Precautions with tables

Before concluding this chapter, we must caution you on the use of tables. COBOL's table-building and table-handling facilities are *very* powerful, and you will soon discover they are so useful that they are nearly indispensable for most non-trivial applications. Unfortunately, tables have a Jekyll-and-Hyde characteristic to them — they are a likely spot for bugs in your code.

Perhaps the most common problem is the so-called boundary problem. COBOL assumes that if we reference the 4,265th entry in a table that was defined in the DATA DIVISION as only ten entries long, we must know what we are doing; it therefore allows us to proceed. The normal result is that our program aborts, and we are left wondering what went wrong.

The obvious moral: Whenever you finish coding a program that makes use of a table, inspect the code for possible boundary errors. Ask yourself if it is possible for your program to set the index or subscript to a value one greater or one less than the number of entries in the table? If so, what will happen? Similarly, ask yourself what happens if the program does *not* find a match in a table lookup? If you assume that such a situation will never occur, you are leaving yourself open for problems.

Your code should always include an "if table exhausted" clause along with the "if match found" clause. The following pseudocode is the basic form for every table lookup:

```
PERFORM table-lookup
    VARYING index
        FROM first-entry BY one-entry
        UNTIL entry (index) = element
            OR no-more-entries.
IF entry (index) = element
    THEN found-match
ELSE
    THEN no-match-in-entire-table.
```

or

SEARCH table-entries VARYING index
    AT END
        there-was-no-match
    WHEN
        there-is-a-match.
IF there-was-a-match

ELSE no-match

    ----------.

or

SEARCH ALL table-entries
    AT END
        there-was-no-match
    WHEN
        there-was-a-match.
IF there-was-a-match

ELSE

    ----------.

12 Advanced Input-Output Techniques

12.1 IDENTIFICATION DIVISION options

In this chapter, we discuss how a COBOL program interfaces with the operating system, and how this makes your work as a programmer much easier. We also discuss several COBOL options which simplify input-output (or I/O for short) no matter how a file is organized. The chapter concludes with remarks about two special COBOL features: teleprocessing (or data communications) and the report writer facility.

Before beginning the I/O discussion, let's take a look at the various options available when using the IDENTIFICATION DIVISION. All of our programs include the PROGRAM-ID paragraph because it *must* appear in every program. The AUTHOR paragraph, plus several other IDENTIFICATION DIVISION paragraphs, are optional; however, your data processing organization may have standards requiring you to include them in your program.

Aside from the PROGRAM-ID paragraph, COBOL treats other IDENTIFICATION DIVISION paragraphs as comments in the program. You, therefore, may want to check their accuracy very carefully, since COBOL won't. An example of a typical IDENTIFICATION DIVISION follows:

```
IDENTIFICATION DIVISION.
PROGRAM-ID. COMPTAX.
AUTHOR. MY NAME.
INSTALLATION. CORP-HEADQRTRS.
DATE-WRITTEN. 10-17-77.
DATE-COMPILED.
SECURITY. PAYROLL CLEARANCE NECESSARY.
```

The DATE-COMPILED clause is left blank when you write your program, because the COBOL compiler automatically will insert the current date each time the program is compiled. This is a very useful feature, since it may help you to determine whether you are reading the current version of a program or an obsolete version. Occasionally, a programmer will forget to replace an obsolete version of a program source listing with the most recent one — and, as a result, often spends frustrating hours debugging the wrong version of the program. This error may be caught if the DATE-COMPILED entry is suspiciously old. Most data processing organizations demand that DATE-COMPILED be included for just that reason.

12.2 ENVIRONMENT DIVISION options

The CONFIGURATION SECTION provides a place to designate the type of computer on which your program is to be compiled and executed. For example, we could code

```
ENVIRONMENT DIVISION.
CONFIGURATION SECTION.
SOURCE-COMPUTER. IBM-370.
OBJECT-COMPUTER. IBM-370.
```

The SOURCE-COMPUTER clause indicates which computer will be used to compile your program, while OBJECT-COMPUTER specifies the computer on which the program will be executed.

As with the IDENTIFICATION DIVISION, these clauses in the ENVIRONMENT DIVISION are optional and may be treated as comments by your particular COBOL compiler. Consequently, the ENVIRONMENT DIVISION options often are overlooked by programmers since they neither define nor operate upon data. However, these options contain information for which many a programmer is thankful when he is responsible for changing the code in an alien program — that is, a program coded by someone who is no longer around to explain what the program does. So, follow your organization's COBOL standards for the IDENTIFICATION DIVISION and for the ENVIRONMENT DIVISION.

12.3 Options of the OPEN and CLOSE statements

The variations of both the OPEN and CLOSE statements depend largely on the physical file-storage medium. For example, the possibilities for handling a magnetic tape (on which records usually can be accessed only in a sequential fashion) are vastly different from the options for manipulating a disk (on which records can be accessed sequentially, randomly, or directly). In Section 12.5, we'll learn more about accessing records from a disk file, but, first, let's look at the various ways of OPENing a file that resides on magnetic tape.

A standard OPEN statement for a magnetic tape file positions the tape so that the first record on the tape is accessed when the first READ statement in the program is executed. Subsequent READ statements will access the second, third, fourth, and following records in an obvious fashion. For many common EDP applications, this approach is sufficient: Each record in a file has to be printed in a report, or processed to produce paychecks, or examined to see whether processing is necessary.

Sometimes, though, our processing is not so straightforward — and, for unusual applications, COBOL provides an OPEN REVERSED statement. As the name implies, it positions the tape so that the first READ statement in the program selects the *last* record in the file, with subsequent READs producing the immediately previous record.

Why would anyone want to read a tape backwards? As an example, suppose we had a tape file containing customer information, with each record having a unique five-digit customer number. It happens that all government agencies with which we do business have account numbers beginning with 99 — e.g., 99001, 99002, and so forth. Let's also imagine that the file is sequenced in ascending order by customer number, and that we have several thousand customers on the file. Now, suppose that we wish to create a listing of all the government agencies, without any particular regard for the actual sequence of customer numbers. We could OPEN the file in the normal fashion and read through all of the customer records until we finally found one with a customer number starting with 99. Or, if it is important that our program execute relatively quickly, we could OPEN the file in a REVERSED fashion, and begin printing the government agencies immediately.

Here's how we code the REVERSED option:

OPEN INPUT CUST-FILE REVERSED.

In this case, the end-of-file condition is handled in the same way as for normal READ operations, except that the AT END clause is activated when a READ is attempted *after* READing the physically first record on the file.

Just as there are various options on opening a file, so are there options for closing the file. A simple CLOSE statement will cause a magnetic tape file to be rewound. (This usually occurs for the convenience of the computer operator, who will remove the tape file from the magnetic tape drive.) However, the CLOSE statement also has the advantage of physically positioning the file so that another program can efficiently OPEN the same file (i.e., the OPEN statement will find that the file has already been positioned at the first record) and begin reading it.

It is possible — and sometimes desirable — to CLOSE WITH NO REWIND. As you would expect, this statement closes the file, and leaves the tape exactly where it was at the time of the CLOSE. Normally, this is used in situations in which one program will CLOSE a file WITH NO REWIND and a subsequent program will OPEN the file REVERSED. To code such a CLOSE statement, we could write:

CLOSE CUST-FILE WITH NO REWIND.

There is an important option that can be used to CLOSE any type of file: the WITH LOCK option. When a file is CLOSEd WITH LOCK, no matter how the program runs, that file cannot be OPENed again during the execution of the program that issued

132 LEARNING TO PROGRAM IN STRUCTURED COBOL

the CLOSE. This prevents the file from being reopened and overwritten if a bug exists in your program.

12.4 Buffering and blocking

So far, we have talked about records without saying very much about the actual manner in which they are stored on a tape or disk, or the actual manner in which the computer reads the records from the I/O device and provides them to your program. These physical details, which we've left for late in the book, often can have an important effect on the efficiency of your program. The two major concepts to be discussed in this section are *blocking* and *buffering*.

Records are stored on tape or disk in blocks. In the case of disks, the blocks are usually of a fixed maximum size — some disks have 512-character blocks, while others have 3,844-character blocks. With magnetic tapes, however, the blocks can be as long or as short as the situation requires — although it is customary for all blocks on the same tape to be the same length.

On a magnetic tape, a block is really just a contiguous group of records; the blocks are separated by interrecord gaps, which are the lengths of blank tape that signal the computer when one block has ended and another is about to begin. Since the interrecord gaps take up space on the tape (typically, 3/4 inch), it is more economical to use blocks that are relatively large compared to the interrecord gaps.

If, for example, we stored only about 200 characters of data in each block, we probably would find that about 50 percent of the available space on the tape was being used up by interrecord gaps (the precise figures depend on such things as the *recording density* used to record data on the tape, and other physical characteristics that may vary from one hardware manufacturer's tape drive to another's).

We have implied that when a READ statement is executed, a record magically is read from the tape or disk file and is brought into an area of memory (typically called a *buffer)*, where it is made available to the program. While that explanation was sufficient before, we now should point out that it only *appears* to work that way. Actually, a number of records are grouped into one block. Each block is considered a *physical record* by the operating system, while each record referenced with a READ statement is called a *logical record.* Operating systems work with physical records; programs work with logical records.

The number of logical records in a block (or physical record) is stated in the BLOCK CONTAINS *n* RECORDS clause of a file's FD. Alternatively, the number may be part of the information contained in the Job Control Language (JCL) provided with your program in order to tell the operating system how to run your program.

When a file is OPENed, two areas — or buffers — are set up to receive records from a file. Each buffer is large enough to hold one physical record. Then, as part of the OPEN statement, the first two physical records are read into the buffers. When a READ statement is executed, the first logical record contained within the first physical record is made available to the program.

As subsequent READing is done, the first physical record is exhausted — and the next READ automatically will receive the first logical record in the second buffer. This switch of buffers also triggers the actual reading of the next physical record into the first buffer, overlaying the records previously used by the program. To the programmer, the records appear to be coming into memory one after the other from the input-output device; in fact, the input is accomplished asynchronously with the READ commands.

With sequential files, WRITE statements work in exactly the same way. Every time a WRITE is executed, a logical record is appended to the current physical record in a buffer. When a physical record has been composed from the appropriate number of logical records, the operating system begins writing the physical record, and simultaneously switches to the other buffer for assembly of the next physical record.

What if we were READing or WRITEing records in blocks of 20, but our file had only 15 logical records? Let's examine these two cases separately. If we were READing, the last block (or physical record) would contain only 15 logical records. Therefore, when we attempted to READ the sixteenth record (which doesn't exist), our program would get an end-of-file indication. Thus, we don't need to organize our file in such a way as to guarantee that the number of logical records is an exact multiple of the number of physical records — the last physical record can be short, without affecting our programming.

If we were WRITEing, the last physical record would not be complete — it, too, would contain only 15 logical records, and the last block automatically would be written to the I/O device when the CLOSE statement for the file was executed.

In almost all programs, two buffers are sufficient to accomplish efficient overlapping of input-output and actual processing — that is, a program will work on the logical records in one buffer while the operating system is doing the physical input-output in another buffer.

In special situations requiring more than two buffers, the RESERVE *n* ALTERNATE AREAS clause can be used with the SELECT statement, with *n* specifying the number of buffers needed *in addition to* the one buffer which a program must have if it is to accomplish any input-output.

By specifying RESERVE NO ALTERNATE AREAS, you can ensure that only one buffer will be set up for your file. While this will save a certain amount of memory (how much memory depends on the size of your physical records), it generally will slow your program — simply because your program will be forced to wait while the next physical record is read into or written out of the buffer. Similarly, reserving more than one alternate buffer will increase the amount of memory your program consumes, but it may speed up your program.

It is likely that your data processing organization has guidelines for blocking factors — specifying, for example, how many logical records should be contained in a physical record — and for buffering. Before you decide to increase or decrease the number of buffers or the block size, you should consult those guidelines.

12.5 Indexed input-output

Thus far in this chapter, we have been concerned with sequential access of records. Although this is the most common method used in business data processing applications, it does have its limitations: In order to look at one specific record, it is necessary to READ each preceding record, even though those records are of no interest to us. This process can be quite time-consuming — especially since files used in today's computer systems frequently contain more than a million records.

Direct access into a file for a specific record can be accomplished by using *indexed* organization.[1] This is specified in the SELECT statement with the ORGANIZATION IS INDEXED clause. (A small but important reminder: You cannot arbitrarily change the organization of a file. When the file is created, it is given a certain organization that remains constant for the file's lifetime.) Along with the ORGANIZATION clause, a RECORD KEY IS clause must be specified to indicate which field will act as a pointer to a specific record in the file.

For example, let's suppose that we want to access directly a client on the charter tour customer file. Assuming that each client has a unique customer number, we could write RECORD KEY IS CLIENT-NUMBER. This indexed file organization would allow us to access any customer by CLIENT-NUMBER. Or, if we state in the SELECT statement that ACCESS MODE IS SEQUENTIAL, we could retrieve clients in the order in which the file is organized, from the first record to the last record (i.e., just as if it were a magnetic tape file).

---

[1] For more information on indexed file organization, see *Learning to Program in Structured COBOL, Part 1*, Section 7.4.

COBOL also provides an alternate path into a file when using indexed I/O. By using the ALTERNATE RECORD KEY IS clause in the SELECT statement, a specific record in the charter tour system could be accessed by, say, the customer phone number.

In addition to allowing a second direct path into a file, the ALTERNATE RECORD KEY is very useful for accessing groups of records whose key fields have the same value. Unlike the key stated in the RECORD KEY IS clause (often known as the prime key), the ALTERNATE RECORD KEY may be a field that does not have a unique value in each record.

In the charter tour system, for example, there might be multiple records with the same tour number; this could be coded as ALTERNATE RECORD KEY IS TOUR-NUMBER WITH DUPLICATES. This permits us to access directly the first record with a specific tour number, then all of the rest of the records with the identical tour number. If a request is made for all clients booked on tour 16872, we need not read through *all* of the client records testing each one for the requested tour.

The entire SELECT statement for the client file might be something like this:

```
SELECT CUST-FILE
    ASSIGN TO UT-I-SYS001
    ORGANIZATION IS INDEXED
    ACCESS MODE IS DYNAMIC
*THIS ALLOWS BOTH INDEXED AND SEQUENTIAL ACCESS
    RECORD KEY IS CLIENT-NUMBER
    ALTERNATE RECORD KEY IS TOUR-NUMBER WITH DUPLICATES.
```

Additional verbs besides READ and WRITE have the ability to access records directly. For example, we can code

```
DELETE CUST-FILE RECORD
    INVALID KEY
        DISPLAY 'RECORD ' CLIENT-NUMBER ' NOT THERE'
        UPON CONSOLE.
```

This deletes the record corresponding to the key at the time of the DELETE statement. If there is no corresponding record, and the access mode is not sequential, then the INVALID KEY clause will be activated.

Or, we can write

READ CUST-FILE NEXT RECORD.

When we have specified a dynamic access mode in our SELECT statement, the NEXT RECORD clause permits retrieval of the *next* record asynchronously with the record currently being processed. That is, input is done in a buffered fashion as if READing were being done sequentially.

We can also code

REWRITE CUST-RECD.

This will cause the specified record to be written back onto the disk in its original place. This particular technique is called updating in place.

Finally, we can code

$$\text{START CUST} - \text{FILE KEY} \begin{cases} \text{IS EQUAL TO} \\ \text{IS GREATER THAN} \\ \text{IS NOT LESS THAN} \end{cases} \text{field} - \text{name}$$

This will position the file so that the pointer locates the first record that satisfies the condition.

12.6 Relative input-output

Relative I/O is another organization which permits either sequential or direct access. As with indexed I/O, it is necessary to have a key to access a relative file. However, the similarity ends there. An indexed file requires that each record have a unique value for its key field, while a relative file does not depend on any field value.

Instead, the relative file works with a key based on relative position of a record in the file. If the RELATIVE KEY field is equal to 50, the record in the fiftieth slot is returned, regardless of whether record slots 01 through 49 contain any records. This permits direct access for files that do not have a natural key field within every record. We would code this as follows:

```
SELECT CUST-FILE
    ASSIGN TO UT-R-SYS001
    ORGANIZATION IS RELATIVE
                        (SEQUENTIAL
    ACCESS MODE IS      {RANDOM          }  , RELATIVE KEY IS R-POINTER
                        (DYNAMIC
```

As shown in the code above, there are three possible access modes: SEQUENTIAL, which allows access of one record after another from the first to the last; RANDOM, which permits access only by RELATIVE KEY; and DYNAMIC, which permits RANDOM and SEQUENTIAL access.

We can use the same verbs for accessing relative files that we use for accessing indexed files: READ, WRITE, DELETE, REWRITE, and START.

12.7 File status

There is another aspect of the physical world that we need to discuss: the possibility of errors and unusual, unanticipated situations when doing I/O. It is possible (although not common) that our COBOL program will be unsuccessful in its attempt to OPEN, CLOSE, READ, START, WRITE, or REWRITE. Unless we specify a suitable action, our program will abort if an error is detected on any of these I/O operations. In many cases, this is unnecessary: Processing often can continue (with, perhaps, the erroneous record being deleted or ignored) once the error is detected, noted on an error report, and circumvented. This is particularly true of programs that may run for hours while processing hundreds of thousands of I/O operations. It is impractical and inefficient to let one I/O error abort the entire job.

To check the success or failure of an I/O operation, COBOL offers the FILE STATUS IS clause in the SELECT statement. For example, we could code

FILE STATUS IS CUST-INDICATOR.

CUST-INDICATOR must be a two-position alphanumeric field defined by the programmer; consequently, it can have a name chosen by the programmer. Each of the two positions contains useful information concerning the status of the file, which we typically will want to examine *after* an I/O operation has been executed. It is convenient to refer to the left-most position of CUST-INDICATOR as key 1, and the right-most position as key 2.

For *sequentially organized* files, key 1 will have the following values and meanings:

'0'	-	successful I/O operation
'1'	-	end of file reached
'3'	-	permanent error
'9'	-	defined by the computer vendor

Key 2 contains the following information:

'0'	-	no further information
'4'	-	when key 1 = '3', an attempt was made to use more space than was allocated by the operating system

When key 1 = '9', key 2 contains values that have been defined by the computer vendor.

For *relative organization,* key 1 has the following values:

'0'	-	successful I/O operation
'1'	-	end of file reached
'2'	-	invalid key
'3'	-	permanent error
'9'	-	defined by the computer vendor

If key 1 = '9', key 2 will be defined by the computer vendor. However, if key 1 = '2', key 2 provides more information about the nature of the invalid key error. In this case, the possible values for key 2 are:

'0'	-	no further information
'2'	-	an attempt was made to write a record that would have created a duplicate key
'3'	-	no record found
'4'	-	an attempt was made to write beyond the defined boundaries of the file

If *indexed organization* is used, the values of key 1 can be '0', '1', '2', '3', or '9'; the meaning of these values is exactly the same as for relative file organization. However, the details regarding key 2 vary slightly.

If key 1 = '0' and key 2 = '0', then the I/O operation was successful, and the operating system has no further information to provide. However, if key 1 = '0' and key 2 = '2', then *either* a duplicate key has just been written (or rewritten) for the alternate key value, *or* if a READ has just been executed, then the record just read and the *next* record have duplicate keys.

If key 1 = '2', an invalid key situation has occurred. In this case, key 2 will be coded as follows:

'1'	-	a sequence error has occurred when the indexed file was being accessed sequentially (records must be in ascending order by record key)
'2'	-	an attempt was made to write or rewrite a record that would have caused a duplicate key to be created
'3'	-	no record on the file has the specified key
'4'	-	ran out of space

Use of the keys enables you to continue running your program even though an I/O operation has failed. However, testing key values after each I/O operation can be tedious as well as awkward. Fortunately, the task is simplified considerably by the USE statement, detailed in Section 12.8 below.

12.8 The USE statement and DECLARATIVES section

We now know that COBOL makes it possible to determine whether an I/O error has occurred. In most programs, we can specify the type of error-checking that is to be carried out in the DECLARATIVES. DECLARATIVES must immediately follow the PROCEDURE DIVISION statement and must end with the sentence END DECLARATIVES. For example, we might code

```
PROCEDURE DIVISION.
DECLARATIVES.
section-name SECTION.
USE statement.
    .
    .
    .
END DECLARATIVES.
```

Within the DECLARATIVES section the USE statement defines the particular conditions under which the error-handling routines should be executed.

The most common form of USE statement is

USE AFTER STANDARD ERROR PROCEDURE ON CUST-FILE.

Instructions for handling *any* I/O error for the CUST-FILE follow this statement; together, these statements comprise an entire *section* of code within the DECLARATIVES part of the program.

Since you may have several files, you may need several USE statements, each with its own section of error-handling code. It is also possible to have USE statements for input, output, or I/O, rather than for specific files, although this is less common.

Control automatically will pass to the DECLARATIVES when an error is encountered; control will return to the statement following the I/O statement when the END DECLARATIVES is encountered (or, in most cases, when the appropriate USE statement or statements have been executed). That is, the program operates just as if you had written the following code, using the DECLARATIVES:

```
READ CUST-FILE
    IF ANY ERROR FOUND
        PERFORM DECLARATIVES.
```

instead of writing

```
READ CUST-FILE.
```

If, for some reason, you want to have the DECLARATIVES handle end-of-file conditions, all you need do is omit the AT END clause on READ statements. Control automatically will pass to DECLARATIVES when end of file is found. If a program contains both DECLARATIVES and AT END, the AT END clause takes precedence over DECLARATIVES.

12.9 Introduction to Report Writer and Data Communications

There are two special features of COBOL that rarely are used because of their complex qualities: the Report Writer feature and the Data Communications feature. The Report Writer allows the programmer to code the report layout in the DATA DIVISION in such a way that COBOL automatically will accomplish most of the work of writing the reports without any coding in the PROCEDURE DIVISION.

Within the DATA DIVISION, the *Record Description* (RD) is defined in much the same way that an FD is defined. The Report Writer can handle page counting, accumulating of totals, detail line formatting, heading and footing titles, and much more. (We will make no attempt in this book to teach you the intricacies of the Report Writer — that would take a book in itself![2] If your organization uses this feature, refer to your COBOL manual for a thorough description.)

COBOL uses the Data Communications feature to deal with the special situations of teleprocessing. There are many problems that may arise when messages (input transactions) enter a system from remote terminals. The Data Communications feature, along with a message control system, provides COBOL with the ability to handle this situation. The feature is complex and seldom used, since teleprocessing systems rarely are written in COBOL.

12.10 Benefits of an operating system

Many of the topics discussed in this chapter will affect you only indirectly, since the operating system will allocate buffers as well as read from and write to the files.

Operating systems are resident (always in the computer) programs, built specifically to make the job of writing and executing application programs easier. They operate like black boxes, since the COBOL programmer need not know how the operating system actually handles details — all he needs to know is that the input or output is actually accomplished when a READ or WRITE is executed.

---

[2]Relatively few versions of COBOL actually have implemented the Report Writer, and *very* few organizations use it. Hence, our decision not to elaborate on this aspect of COBOL.

When a COBOL program is to be run, special instructions can be given to the program via the operating system's Job Control Language. The JCL usually supplies information to the operating system about what files will be needed by the program, what files will be created, how much space on a storage medium a new file will require, which files should be saved at the completion of the program's execution, which files should be deleted, and how much memory the program will require.

All of this information is used by the operating system to help schedule the job, and to help manage the resources of the entire computer system as efficiently as possible (because, generally, several programs are executing on the computer at the same time). The operating system will not load the program into memory if there are not enough storage devices available to READ and WRITE all of the files. This scheduling — completely hidden from the programmer — helps make the computer operate in a more cost-effective way. It also allows the application programmer to concentrate on solving the business problem rather than playing with the hardware.

There are many different types of operating systems, but they all have the same basic purpose: to let the programmer worry about solving the problem, while leaving the operating system free to handle the details of making good use of the particular computer hardware.

13 Sorting and Merging

13.1 Introduction

Sorting and *merging* are two related procedures that are used frequently by COBOL programmers. Sorting involves the automatic ordering of records under a programmer's direction; merging involves the interleaving of several files into one ordered sequence of records.

Sorting and merging can be accomplished with a single key field, or multiple key fields. For example, the customer records for the charter tour system could be sorted into ascending sequence on CLIENT-NUMBER; or it might be useful to sort these records into ascending sequence on TOUR-NUMBER, and within each tour, into ascending order on CLIENT-NUMBER. Both of these sorts can be accomplished with a single SORT statement.

13.2 The SORT statement

Let's begin by looking at a small, simple program which accomplishes a SORT, shown in the code on the following page.

The program sorts the customer file into ascending TOUR-NUMBER order — and, within that, ascending CLIENT-NUMBER order. In case you think the program is wrong because it lacks OPENs and CLOSEs, don't worry — the SORT automatically OPENs and CLOSEs the files.

The key fields are listed in order from major to minor; we can request ascending or descending sequencing to be done for each. The program uses numeric fields for keys, but the sort can be used with non-numeric keys as well. Sorting into ascending sequence with an alpha field key would produce a file in alphabetic order by key field. As is evident from the code, the USING clause on the SORT statement names the unsorted input file, and the GIVING clause names the sorted file that will be the output.

```
IDENTIFICATION DIVISION.
PROGRAM-ID. SIMPLSRT.

ENVIRONMENT DIVISION.

INPUT-OUTPUT SECTION.
FILE-CONTROL.
    SELECT CUST-FILE-IN ASSIGN TO UT-S-MSTTAPE.
    SELECT CUST-SORT ASSIGN TO DA-S-WORKROOM.
    SELECT CUST-FILE-OUT ASSIGN TO UT-S-NEWTAPE.

DATA DIVISION.
FD  CUST-FILE-IN
    LABEL RECORDS ARE STANDARD
    RECORD CONTAINS 120 CHARACTERS
    BLOCK CONTAINS 0 RECORDS
    DATA RECORD IS OLD-CUST.
01  OLD-CUST                 PIC X(120).
SD  CUST-SORT
    RECORD CONTAINS 120 CHARACTERS
    DATA RECORD IS SORT-CUST.
01  SORT-CUST.
    05  TOUR-NUMBER          PIC 9(5).
    05  CLIENT-NUMBER        PIC 9(5).
    05  FILLER               PIC X(110).
FD  CUST-FILE-OUT
    LABEL RECORDS ARE STANDARD
    RECORD CONTAINS 120 CHARACTERS
    BLOCK CONTAINS 0 RECORDS
    DATA RECORD IS NEW-CUST.
01  NEW-CUST                 PIC X(120).

PROCEDURE DIVISION.
SORT-CUSTOMERS.
    SORT CUST-SORT
        ON ASCENDING KEY TOUR-NUMBER
        ON ASCENDING KEY CLIENT-NUMBER
        USING CUST-FILE-IN
        GIVING CUST-FILE-OUT.
    STOP RUN.
```

13.3 The SORT description (SD)

In the coding example in Section 13.2, we named an *inter-mediate* file, CUST-SORT, to be used as a work space during the process of ordering the records. A file is considered to be inter-mediate when it is created *within* the program (i.e., it did not ex-ist before the program began running, in contrast to a *permanent* file), and when it is of no further use at the conclusion of the program's execution.

The COBOL SORT requires work space in order to shuffle the records into the requested sequence. Note that CUST-SORT is assigned a disk with its own SELECT statement. This work file is described by what appears to be a normal file description — ex-cept that instead of calling it an FD, we call it a SORT description. The SD and the corresponding record layout describe each record's appearance as it goes into the SORT. The key fields for the sorting sequence must be defined in a record description at-tached to an SD.

13.4 INPUT and OUTPUT PROCEDUREs

The example shown in Section 13.2 does nothing more than sort the file. However, COBOL permits the programmer to reference and manipulate both the input to the SORT, and the output from it — and, in many cases, the COBOL programmer needs that facility.

If we wish to reference information on a file *before* it is sorted, we use an INPUT PROCEDURE; the INPUT PROCEDURE is declared as part of the SORT statement. Similarly, if we wish to work with sorted records (that is, records that are produced, one at a time, by the sorting mechanism), we declare an OUTPUT PROCEDURE in the SORT statement.

As an example, on the following pages we see a program that selects customers who are flying from a specified airport on a specific date, sorts them by tour and client number, and then prints a listing of these customers:

```
IDENTIFICATION DIVISION.
PROGRAM-ID. FANCYSRT.


ENVIRONMENT DIVISION.

INPUT-OUTPUT SECTION.
FILE-CONTROL.
     SELECT CUST-FILE-IN ASSIGN TO UT-S-MSTTAPE.
     SELECT CUST-SORT ASSIGN TO DA-S-WORKROOM.
     SELECT CONTROL-REC ASSIGN TO UR-S-SYSIN.
     SELECT CUST-LIST ASSIGN TO UR-S-SYSPRINT.


DATA DIVISION.

FILE SECTION.
FD  CUST-FILE-IN
     LABEL RECORDS ARE OMITTED
     RECORD CONTAINS 80 CHARACTERS
     BLOCK CONTAINS 0 RECORDS
     DATA RECORD IS OLD-CUST.
01  OLD-CUST.
     05   FILLER             PIC X(45).
     05   AIR-SELECTED        PIC A(3).
     05   FILLER             PIC X(27).
     05   DEPART-DATE         PIC 9(5).


*
* DEPARTURE DATE IS IN DDDYY FORMAT.
*


SD  CUST-SORT
     RECORD CONTAINS 80 CHARACTERS
     DATA RECORD IS SORTING-CUST.
01  SORTING-CUST.
     05   TOUR-NUMBER         PIC 9(5).
     05   CLIENT-NUMBER       PIC 9(5).
     05   CLIENT-NAME         PIC X(20).
     05   CLIENT-ADDR         PIC X(15).
     05   FILLER             PIC X(3).
     05   BALANCE-DUE         PIC 9(4)V99.
     05   FILLER             PIC X(26).

FD  CUST-LIST
     LABEL RECORDS ARE OMITTED
     RECORD CONTAINS 132 CHARACTERS
     DATA RECORD IS CUSTOMER-LIST.
```

```
01  CUSTOMER-LIST              PIC X(132).

WORKING-STORAGE SECTION.
01  EOF-SORT                   PIC X(3)    VALUE 'NO '.
01  EOF-CUST                   PIC X(3)    VALUE 'NO '.
01  PRINT-LINE.
    05   FILLER                PIC X(2).
    05   TR-NUM                PIC 9(5).
    05   FILLER                PIC X(5).
    05   CL-NUM                PIC 9(5).
    05   FILLER                PIC X(10).
    05   CL-NAME               PIC X(20).
    05   FILLER                PIC X(3).
    05   CL-ADDR               PIC X(15).
    05   FILLER                PIC X(5).
    05   BAL-DUE               PIC $$$$9.99-.
    05   FILLER                PIC X(54).
01  SELECTED-REC.
    05   TOUR-NUMB             PIC 9(5).
    05   CLIENT-NUMB           PIC 9(5).
    05   CLIENT-NAM            PIC X(20).
    05   CLIENT-ADD            PIC X(15).
    05   FILLER                PIC X(3).
    05   BALANCE-DUE           PIC S9(4)V99.
    05   FILLER                PIC X(26).

FD  CONTROL-REC
    LABEL RECORDS ARE OMITTED
    RECORD CONTAINS 80 CHARACTERS
    DATA RECORD IS CONTROL-CARD.
01  CONTROL-CARD.
    05   CONTROL-AIR           PIC A(3).
    05   FILLER                PIC X(6).
    05   CONTROL-DATE          PIC 9(5).
    05   FILLER                PIC X(66).

PROCEDURE DIVISION.

SORT-SELECTED.
    SORT CUST-SORT
        ASCENDING KEY TOUR-NUMBER
        ASCENDING KEY CLIENT-NUMBER
        INPUT PROCEDURE SELECT-CUSTOMERS.
        OUTPUT PROCEDURE CREATE-LIST.
END-SORT.
    EXIT PROGRAM.

SELECT-CUSTOMERS SECTION.
GET-CUSTOMERS.
    OPEN INPUT CUST-FILE-IN
        INPUT CONTROL-CARD.
    PERFORM READ-CONTROL.
    PERFORM READ-CUST.
```

```
      PERFORM SELECT-LOOP
          UNTIL EOF-CUST = 'YES'.
      CLOSE CUST-FILE-IN.
      GO TO SELECT-CUSTOMERS-EXIT.
  SELECT-LOOP.
      IF CONTROL-AIR = AIR-SELECTED
          AND CONTROL-DATE = DEPART-DATE
              MOVE OLD-CUST TO SORTING-CUST
              RELEASE SORTING-CUST.
      PERFORM READ-CUST.
  READ-CUST.
      READ CUST-FILE-IN
          AT END
              MOVE 'YES' TO EOF-CUST.
  READ-CONTROL.
      READ CONTROL-CARD
          AT END
              DISPLAY 'NO CONTROL CARD - RUN STOPPED.'
              STOP RUN.

  * NOTE: IF EOF, THERE WAS NO CONTROL CARD AT ALL, SO
  * JOB IS ABORTED

  SELECT-CUSTOMERS-EXIT.
      EXIT.

  CREATE-LIST SECTION.
  FORMAT-LINES.
      OPEN OUTPUT CUST-LIST.
      PERFORM GET-FROM-SORT.
      PERFORM FORMAT-LOOP UNTIL EOF-SORT = 'YES'.
      CLOSE CUST-LIST.
      GO TO CREATE-LIST-EXIT.
  FORMAT-LOOP.
      MOVE SPACES TO PRINT-LINE.
      MOVE TOUR-NUMBER TO TR-NUM.
      MOVE CLIENT-NUMBER TO CL-NUM.
      MOVE CLIENT-NAME TO CL-NAME.
      MOVE CLIENT-ADDR TO CL-ADDR.
      MOVE BALANCE-DUE TO BAL-DUE.
      PERFORM WRITE-LINE.
      PERFORM GET-FROM-SORT.
  GET-FROM-SORT.
      RETURN CUST-SORT RECORD INTO SELECTED-REC
          AT END MOVE 'YES' TO EOF-SORT.
  WRITE-LINE.
      WRITE CUSTOMER-LIST FROM PRINT-LINE.
  CREATE-LIST-EXIT.
      EXIT.
```

This program looks different from our previous examples, primarily because the rules of the COBOL SORT dictate a special arrangement for the INPUT and OUTPUT PROCEDUREs.

COBOL treats this program as three separate and distinct phases of processing, all of which are controlled by the SORT statement. The first phase, the INPUT PROCEDURE, is given control immediately from the SORT. It OPENs and READs records, and as each record is ready to be sorted, it is "released" to the sorting mechanism with the RELEASE statement. When the INPUT PROCEDURE is finished, it EXITs (usually when an end of file has been detected on the input file); then the second phase — the actual sort — begins.

When the sort is finished, control is passed to the third phase — the OUTPUT PROCEDURE. The OUTPUT PROCEDURE obtains records, one at a time, in a sorted sequence, by executing a RETURN statement. The RETURN statement can be considered a "READ next record from sorted file" statement. When the OUTPUT PROCEDURE is finished, it EXITs, and control is passed to the statement immediately following the SORT statement.

The rules involved with the COBOL SORT may require the programmer to write GO TO statements, as demonstrated in the example above. The rules for INPUT and OUTPUT PROCEDUREs are as follows:

1. The INPUT PROCEDURE must consist of one or more contiguous COBOL SECTIONs. Similarly, the OUTPUT PROCEDURE must be comprised of adjacent SECTIONs.

2. The INPUT PROCEDURE may not invoke or reference a paragraph or section outside the INPUT PROCEDURE itself. Similarly, the OUTPUT PROCEDURE may not invoke any paragraphs or sections outside of itself.

3.   No piece of code outside the INPUT PROCEDURE
or OUTPUT PROCEDURE may refer to a paragraph
inside those procedures.

Because the programmer is forced to use adjacent sections for
each SORT procedure, it may be necessary to use a GO TO statement to pass control to the EXIT paragraph in the procedure.
Normally, we would frown on the use of GO TO statements, but
in this case they are unavoidable.

13.5 The MERGE statement

The COBOL MERGE statement combines two or more
identically sequenced files into one ordered file, as specified by
key fields. Its rules are very similar to the SORT. A typical
MERGE statement follows:

```
MERGE MERGE-MONTHS-FILE
    ON ASCENDING KEY TOUR-NUMBER
    ON ASCENDING KEY CLIENT-NUMBER
    USING     JAN-CUST-FILE
              FEB-CUST-FILE
              MAR-CUST-FILE
              APR-CUST-FILE
              MAY-CUST-FILE
              JUN-CUST-FILE
    GIVING FIRST-HALF-YEAR-FILE.
```

The MERGE-MONTHS file must be defined with an SD, just
like a sort file. The rest of the MERGE rules are the same as the
SORT rules, *except* that only an OUTPUT PROCEDURE is allowed.

14 Testing and Debugging

14.1 Introduction to testing

No matter how carefully you write your code, no matter how sure you are that your code is perfect, you still must actually *test* it on a computer. Without testing, the chances of a bug — even in the simplest code — are very high; and the cost of fixing the bugs (known as debugging) and rerunning the job can be very expensive. It is so easy to inadvertently put a bug in code that even the smallest modification to an existing program deserves to be tested on the computer.

If we are to test our program, we need a collection of *test inputs*. These test inputs will produce some outputs — outputs that we should be able to predict before we begin the testing. It is useless to look at test output without knowing whether the output is the correct response to a particular test input; indeed, in such a situation we usually spend most of our time trying to convince ourselves that the test output looks reasonable.

Our test inputs also must exercise *all* of the modules in a program in order to give us confidence that the test is any measure of the program's correctness. For example, if we were testing a program that edits records and produces valid records and an error report, it would be foolish to use only error-free records or only illegal records as test data. Obviously, we need combinations of both to form a worthy set of test data.

14.2 Walkthroughs

In many situations, a program will abort and stop executing when the first bug is encountered. An attempt to divide by zero, an illegal subscript, or any of a number of other bugs may cause the program to be interrupted by the operating system. In such cases, the programmer usually is forced to find the bug that caused the abnormal termination (or "abend," as it is called on some systems), fix it, and then run the test again.

Unfortunately, another bug may be lurking only a few statements further in the code. Naturally, this causes another abend, another effort to find the bug, another recompilation of the program to fix the bug, and yet another test run. This start-and-stop method of testing — in which only one bug is found in each test run — can be long and arduous, as well as expensive. This is particularly true in data processing organizations in which the programmer has to wait for a day or more to have his program compiled, or his test run executed.

In order to avoid this cumbersome process, many organizations use *code walkthroughs* to eliminate as many bugs as possible *before* the first test run. The code walkthrough consists of a review of the program by other COBOL programmers in an attempt to find bugs before the machine does. After the program has been written, and perhaps after it has been compiled (depending on computer turnaround time), the author of the program distributes copies of the code (i.e., program listings or coding sheets) and program specifications to three or four other programmers, giving them a reasonable period of time to review the code privately. The private review process typically takes only an hour, but it usually is advisable to allow two days to ensure that each of the reviewers will be able to squeeze in an hour of reviewing time among his or her other programming duties.

After each programmer has had a chance to review the code, a meeting — or walkthrough — is held to discuss publicly any bugs that might be present *as well as* any deviations from installation standards, major inefficiencies, or any other aspect of the program which the reviewers feel would make it difficult to maintain or modify. Once the author of the program is shown a bug, discussion of that bug usually stops — it is the responsibility of the author to fix the mistake and conduct another walk-through to convince the reviewers that the bug has indeed been eliminated.

If this seems time-consuming, rest assured that, compara-tively, it's not. Time spent reviewing the code in this fashion generally is *much* less than the amount of time the author of the program would require to find a bug using the start-and-stop method of testing. In addition, the walkthrough process usually finds bugs that the author never would have found in his own testing efforts — bugs that usually cause *very* expensive testing, debugging, and rerunning of the program after it has been put into production. Thus, it is important to realize that *all* code needs to be submitted to this walkthrough process; experience has shown us that just as many bugs lurk in simple modules as in complex ones.

Successful walkthroughs are generally very short — usually 30 minutes long, and rarely as long as 60 minutes. Of necessity, this means that a walkthrough normally is used to review a rela-tively small piece of code — typically, 50-100 statements. Many programmers make the mistake of attempting to review too much code, or of prolonging the walkthrough for two or three hours. In both cases, the walkthroughs become superficial, and some bugs are not found. If a large program is being written, a module-by-module review will produce far better results than will one meeting in which bugs are hunted in a 50-page program.

The walkthrough approach also can be very helpful when developing test data. Reviewers must ask themselves the follow-ing questions: Given a certain specification, is this test data a rigorous test of the code? If the program produces the correct results with this test data, can we assume that the program actu-ally does what it is supposed to do?

Chances are good that as you have been learning to write COBOL programs, you and your fellow students have spent many hours wondering why a program abended, or why it pro-duced such mysterious output. Walkthroughs are merely a slightly more formalized version of those brainstorming sessions — except that they take place *before* the program abends!

14.3 Top-down testing

Testing of a COBOL program can be made easier if the code is tested piece by piece, rather than all at once after the entire program has been written. This approach is known as *incremental testing* because it involves coding and testing one module at a time until the entire program is tested. Written in pseudocode, the strategy could be expressed as

> **Code a module**
> **Test that module**
> **WHILE there are more modules in the program**
> **Code a module**
> **Test that module with those already tested**

Top-down testing is an incremental testing approach that works down from the topmost module to the lowest modules in the hierarchy. The rule of top-down testing is that the main module is always written first, and every subsequent module that is coded is immediately subordinate to one that already has been coded and tested.

The structure chart on the following page illustrates top-down testing. The program reads in records labeled X and Z, and outputs records labeled XY′ and XY″. Using top-down testing, the first module to be coded and tested would be MAIN MODULE. The structure chart shows that MAIN MODULE invokes modules 1, 2, 3, and 4; thus, if we are going to test MAIN MODULE, we must simulate the work of these modules by using *stubs,* or "dummy" modules. A stub is a quick-and-dirty module that does either no processing, or only a minimal amount of processing to simulate the behavior of the *real* module.

Our structure chart indicates that module 4 receives record XY as its input. A stub for module 4 might be a single COBOL paragraph that DISPLAYs the XY record each time it receives control. The information DISPLAYed would be used to verify that

MAIN MODULE is passing control to module 4 at the proper time, and that it is passing the proper values in XY.

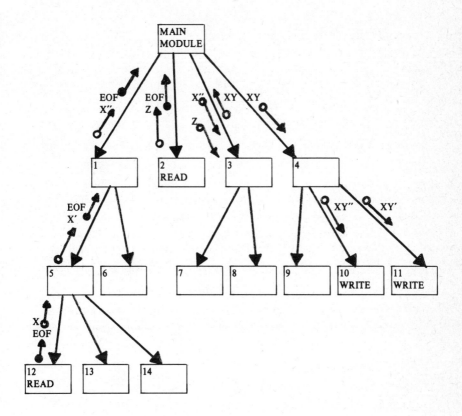

A stub for module 1 is more difficult to code. Somehow, the programmer must simulate a module that returns an X'' record to MAIN MODULE, as well as eventually returning an end-of-file indicator. One possible approach would be to build a table of sample values for X''. The stub for module 1 then could retrieve entries from the table and return them to MAIN MODULE. When the table is exhausted, the stub would return an end-of-file indicator.

Module 3 also could work with a table to return XY records. Or, it could return a constant value of XY, by moving the same value into XY each time it is invoked without regard to the values in X'' and Z. If the programmer decided to return a constant value each time, it would be a good idea to DISPLAY the values of X″ and Z every time the stub is invoked.

Once MAIN MODULE is working, the programmer has a choice of coding and testing modules 1, 2, 3 or 4. The choice generally depends on the programmer's overall implementation strategy for the program. For example, if module 4 is coded, then we could code module 11 immediately afterwards, thereby having our program write out XY′ records long before the program is completely finished.

Alternatively, if module 11 prints out a report, it might be very useful for the user to see an example of the report format. Thus, we might want to start by coding and testing MAIN MODULE, then module 4, and then module 11. If module 11 writes out a file made up of XY′ records, and if some other program in our data processing organization reads those records, then it would be useful to get module 11 working as soon as possible so that we could confirm that the two programs can "talk" to each other.

On the other hand, it may be useful to write module 2 after testing MAIN MODULE. This would mean that we could use a real file of Z records in all subsequent testing. This might be followed by coding modules 1, 5, and 12 in order to be able to use a file of real X records.

The implementation strategy generally will be up to you and the other people involved in the analysis, design, and implementation of your system. The strategy often depends on consideration of whether a primitive version of a system would be useful to the user as a demonstration tool, a training tool, or even as a limited production version of the program. The key to top-down testing is its *incremental* nature: The programmer tests and debugs one piece at a time, rather than writing an entire program and then trying to get all of the modules to work at once.

In the back of the book, there is a structure chart of the program that edits customer records for booking onto flights. The following page shows a strategy for coding and testing the modules of that program in a top-down fashion:

VERSION DESCRIPTION	MODULES WORKING	STUBS
1 This version will write out valid groups exactly as will the finished product; erroneous groups are displayed simply. All editing is simulated.	EDIT-CLIENT TRANSACTIONS GET NEXT VALID GROUP PUT VALID GROUP WRITE A RECORD	GET GROUP CORRECT NUMBER IN GROUP SAME AIRPORTS FORMAT ERROR LIST
2 This version will read in client records, which are assumed to pass all local edits, build clients into groups, check for correct number in a group, check that all members have the same choices for airports, display errors, and write individuals in valid groups.	GET GROUP (CHANGE IN GROUP) CORRECT NUMBER IN GROUP SAME AIRPORTS	FORMAT ERROR LIST GET EDITED CLIENT
3 This version does everything that the final version will do except editing on individual flight information, and on name and address information. It now prints the error listing.	FORMAT ERROR LIST FORMAT HEADER PRINT ERROR LIST	CHECK AIR TRANSPORT INFORMATION CHECK CLIENT INFORMATION
4 This is the production version of the system.	ALL MODULES	

14.4 Common bugs

In this section we will discuss some of the common, garden-variety bugs that creep into almost everyone's programs from time to time. Obviously, the number of possible COBOL mistakes is infinite, so we will confine our discussion to some very common types of errors.

One of the most common bugs is the *data exception:* A program will abort if any field is *defined* in the DATA DIVISION as one type of data, and then *used* in such a way as to cause incompatible types of data to be stored in that field. For example, what would happen if you attempted to add to an accumulator a field containing 'SMITH'. The program would abort with a data exception because arithmetic only can be done with numeric fields.

In many cases, data exceptions occur because the programmer misdefines a record — that is, he accidentally defines one of the fields with an improper length, thereby throwing off the rest of the fields. For example, suppose we have a record which *should* be defined as

```
01   CUSTOMER-RECD.
     05   CUSTOMER-NUMBER     PIC  9(6).
     05   CUSTOMER-NAME       PIC  X(20).
     05   AMT-DUE             PIC  9(4)V99.
```

but, because of a bug, ends up being coded as

```
01   CUSTOMER-RECD.
     05   CUSTOMER-NUMBER     PIC  9(5).
     05   CUSTOMER-NAME       PIC  X(20).
     05   AMT-DUE             PIC  9(4)V99.
```

By misdefining the record, the programmer has caused the following three things to happen:

1. The field CUSTOMER-NAME will include the low-order digit of CUSTOMER-NUMBER. This means that CUSTOMER-NAME probably will contain *alphanumeric* data, which will cause trouble if the program expected it to be purely *alphabetic*.

2. The AMT-DUE field will include the low-order position of the CUSTOMER-NAME field. This means that AMT-DUE probably will end up being alphanumeric instead of pure numeric.

3. The last position of AMT-DUE read in from the file will be dropped, since the *actual* definition of the record is one position less than the amount of data read in.

Under these conditions, it is very likely that the program will abend with a data exception. Indeed, if it doesn't abend, it's pretty obvious that the programmer hasn't implemented very thorough testing! It's very likely, for example, that the program will try to carry out some arithmetic operation on the AMT-DUE field; a data exception will immediately occur, since AMT-DUE generally will contain something like 'R10649'.

There is yet another common cause of data exceptions: failure to initialize WORKING-STORAGE fields that are used as counters or in arithmetic operations. For example, consider the following statement:

ADD 1 TO RECORDS-READ.

This statement could easily cause an abend if the programmer has failed to initialize RECORDS-READ to a numeric value. This happens because COBOL does *not* initialize fields automatically.[1] Instead, the COBOL compiler merely reserves enough space to

---

[1] Actually, fields are initialized to zeroes on some computers — but this is a vendor-dependent feature of which you should definitely *not* take advantage!

hold the field; this means that when your program begins executing, that area of memory usually will contain whatever "garbage" was left behind by the *last* program that occupied that area of memory.

Another common type of COBOL bug, known as "off-by-one errors," can cause different types of abends depending on the specifics of the situation. However, the abends usually are caused by *loops*. For example, when storing entries in a 30-entry table, the programmer may accidentally store 31 entries — thereby overlaying whatever data reside immediately following the thirtieth entry.

Probably the most typical type of off-by-one error is that of iterating through a loop one time too few. To illustrate this, suppose we wanted to count the number of customers we have in each state; let's assume that we've decided to do this with a table lookup using the two-letter state abbreviation. We could cause an off-by-one error by coding

```
PERFORM STATE-COUNTING
    VARYING THIS-STATE FROM 1 BY 1
    UNTIL TABLE-CODE (THIS-STATE) = POSTAL-CODE
        OR THIS-STATE = NUMBER-OF-STATES.
IF THIS-STATE = NUMBER-OF-STATES
    ADD 1 TO FOREIGN-CUSTOMER-COUNTER
ELSE
    ADD 1 TO STATE-COUNTER (THIS-STATE).
```

Presumably, the table with which we are working is NUMBER-OF-STATES entries long. That is, if there are fifty states, we assume that the table has fifty entries, and we assume that NUMBER-OF-STATES has the value of 50. In this case, it turns out that we *never* will match against the last entry in the table (which will be Wyoming, if the table is ordered alphabetically). This is because indexes and subscripts are initialized and incremented *before* the UNTIL clause is tested, and the UNTIL clause is tested *before* the paragraph or section is invoked.

To make this program work the way we want it to, we should have coded

PERFORM STATE-COUNTING
** VARYING THIS-STATE FROM 1 BY 1**
**   UNTIL TABLE-CODE (THIS-STATE) = POSTAL-CODE**
**   OR THIS-STATE GREATER THAN NUMBER-OF-STATES.**

Whenever you write code for a loop, check the conditions of the loop to ensure that:

1. The loop will execute correctly the *first* time it is invoked.

2. The loop is capable of executing *zero* times if that is appropriate — i.e., make sure that your loop can "do nothing gracefully."

3. The loop "will prepare" for the next iteration. In cases where your program is reading input from a sequential file, for example, it is customary to get ready for the next iteration by reading in the next record as the last executable statement at the bottom of the loop.

4. The loop will terminate correctly in *all* possible cases. It is a good idea to work out by hand the details of the *last* iteration of the loop. Check the values of the subscript or index upon conclusion.

Yet another common type of bug is the *limit error*. To illustrate this, let's imagine that you have been asked to write a program that will print one grand-total amount-due figure by summing the outstanding balances of all of the customers of your company. Each customer has a record on a master file, and the amount-due field is a six-position field in the form $$$$¢¢. How large should we make the accumulator that will hold the grand total in our program?

The answer is, *we don't know!* It depends on how many customers there are in the file. When defining counters and accumulators, we need to know the volume our program will be expected to handle. If, for example, we are told that the master file contains ten customer records, we can calculate the minimum size for the accumulator by multiplying the largest possible value in any one occurrence by the number of occurrences. In our example with grand totals, we would compute

$$9999.99 \times 10 = 99999.90$$

Thus, our accumulator *could* be defined as

01   TOTAL-AMT   PIC S9(5)V99   COMP-3.

When defining accumulators, it is far better to assume that every occurrence of a data item that will be added into the accumulator will have its *largest* possible value, rather than an estimated *average* value.

What if the master file in our example has an eleventh customer added to it? Then, it is possible that the grand total could be as large as

$$9999.99 \times 11 = 109999.89$$

Now the accumulator defined as S9(5)V99 may not be large enough to hold the grand total. Consequently, we may encounter a SIZE ERROR when the program is executed; that is, the program will abend with a message telling us that we tried to store a value too large for the field. This means that the accumulator will have to be redefined (perhaps as an S9(7)V99 field); the program will have to be recompiled, and the job will have to be rerun.

Obviously, another factor that we should take into account when defining accumulators is the likelihood that the user will expand the number of items to be summed. If it is possible for such an expansion to take place, it is sensible to build in some surplus capacity in the accumulators — after all, it generally only requires one or two more positions of memory.

Remembering that IBM COBOL arithmetic is done on packed decimal numbers (COMP-3), we can compute a reasonable size for accumulators and counters with the formula

(largest possible value of field) ×
(number of fields, rounded up to next order of magnitude) =
(number which must fit in planned accumulator)

If the formula indicates that the accumulator should have an even number of positions, add an extra high-order position — since COBOL will do it anyway for COMP-3 fields.

Here is an example. Suppose we have to accumulate a total of 65 two-position numeric fields. We would compute

$$99 \times 100 = 9900$$

(Note that we rounded 65 up to the next higher order of magnitude.) Since the smallest field that could hold 9900 would be four positions in length, we add one more position, and define our accumulator as follows:

```
01  ACCUMULATOR       PIC S9(5)   COMP-3.
```

14.5 Debugging strategies and techniques

By the time you have gotten to this section, debugging probably will have become a familiar task to you. For most programmers, it is a painful and exasperating task, which consumes hours of checking page after page of code . . . only to discover that the bug was a simple coding blunder. For many programmers, debugging is the blackest of the black magic of programming — yet, it does not have to be such a tortuous task.

The most helpful technique in debugging is to *localize* the bug to a small area of the program. One way of accomplishing this is to remember to *never* attempt to test all of the modules in a COBOL program in one fell swoop. By designing modules that are small and well-defined, and by testing the program in a top-down incremental fashion, you should be able to tell which piece of your program contains the bug that has just caused the entire program to abend.

For example, suppose we have designed a 50-module program. If we compile all 50 modules at once, develop test data for the entire program, run the test, and discover a data exception, we probably will be faced with a rather difficult debugging task. The bug might be in any one of the 50 modules. However, if we run several small tests, each one involving the substitution of a new module for its stub, it is reasonable to expect that a data exception will be located much more quickly.

Once you have localized a bug, you should spend about half an hour looking for it. In general, it is more efficient to look at the source code and the actual program output than to look at octal or hexadecimal memory dumps of the program. If you have not found the bug after 30 minutes, it most certainly is time to call for help.

Find one or two other programmers and, with the listing in front of you, describe the problem to your colleagues. Describe why you think the bug is in the area of code that you are examining, and then walk through the code, line by line, explaining how it works. There is an excellent chance that you will discover the bug yourself — your friends won't even have to open their mouths! In other situations, your friends will point out an obvious bug that escaped your attention — after all, since you were the one who put the bug in the program, it is not surprising that you would continue to think that the logic of your program is correct!

Only as a last resort should you make extensive use of the dump, or trace, facilities that most computer systems have. These packages generally produce vast amounts of paper in which only a tiny amount of useful information is found. It is not surprising to see a programmer produce 200 pages of memory dump printout, only to find that one position of memory was initialized incorrectly. If you *must* use dumps, use them sparingly. Typically, the following types of dumps will be more than sufficient to find even the most elusive bugs:

1. A trace that shows the order in which para-graphs, sections, or subprograms were called. This can usually be invoked as part of a debug-ging option found in many COBOL systems; if not, you can do it yourself by having each module DISPLAY a message as the first execut-able statement. Merely by watching the se-quence in which modules are called (and by comparing that with the structure chart that you have developed for the program), you can find many of your bugs.

2. A trace that shows the input parameters passed to each module and the output parameters re-turned from each module. This is most practi-cal when your modules consist of CALLable subprograms; what you want to do is dump the fields defined in the LINKAGE SECTION upon entering each CALLed program, and just prior to exiting. As you can imagine, this produces voluminous output; however, it may be useful in locating a subtle bug that involves the clobbering of certain fields of data.

3. A trace that shows all of the references to and/or all of the modifications to a specified field of data. This approach is usually practical only if you have a debugging package that al-lows you automatically to invoke the tracing of a field. It would generally be very impractical for you to insert your own debugging code to DISPLAY a message every time a field is refer-

enced (and it may not solve the problem — it may turn out that your field of data is being clobbered because of an off-by-one error that you can't even see). Again, this approach can produce voluminous output and should be avoided if possible. More important, try to avoid a shotgun approach of tracing *all* variables in your program — it will produce more output than you would believe possible!

15 Efficiency and Optimization

15.1 Introduction

From time to time we've mentioned that one programming approach is "more efficient" than another approach. But we've generally said very little about efficiency — and you may have gotten the impression that we aren't particularly concerned about the subject.

To the contrary, we are and *should* be concerned about efficiency. Indeed, efficiency is *so* important that we've saved it for last — *after* we've discussed such basic issues as data representations, table-handling, and input-output operations. Now that you're familiar with all of these COBOL techniques, we can talk about ways of making your program more efficient.

But before we begin, we should ask ourselves some simple questions: What does "efficiency" mean? Does it mean a program that consumes very little CPU time? Does it mean a program that requires very little memory? Or does it imply one that makes very few disk accesses?

It's easy to become overly concerned with one or two narrow views of efficiency. In the final analysis, an efficient program is one that minimizes *total* costs, whether measured in dollars, francs, or rubles, over its entire productive lifetime. Total costs include the cost to develop the program, the cost to run it in a production environment (including the cost of reruns), and the cost of maintaining and modifying the program. Our main topic of discussion in this chapter is that of minimizing the cost of *running* the program.

The cost of running a program is becoming a smaller and smaller fraction of the total budget. There's no mystery behind this — it's simply that the price of computer hardware has dropped sharply during the past twenty years (and is expected to continue dropping for the foreseeable future), while the cost of the *people* who design, code, operate, and maintain the programs has increased (and is expected to continue increasing).

In the mid-1970's, for example, most large data processing organizations found that they spent roughly 50 percent of their budgets on hardware, and the other 50 percent on people-related costs. By the mid-1980's, those same organizations expect to spend only 20 percent on hardware, and 80 percent on people-related costs. Thus, the emphasis is shifting much more to minimizing *people* costs, rather than minimizing *hardware* costs. As a result, it often turns out to be more efficient to computerize a manual system even when the computer hardware is idle 98 percent of the time.

There is one aspect of the trade-off between people costs and hardware costs that needs to be discussed more fully. Except for some relatively trivial techniques for improving the hardware efficiency of a program, we usually find that attempts to make a program *very* efficient also make it considerably harder to develop, understand, debug, and maintain.[1] Thus, as we attempt to *decrease* hardware costs, we often find that we have *increased* people costs.

So, what should we conclude from all of this? *While you are writing the program, don't worry about efficiency.* After the program is operational, you can worry about optimizing it. After all, it's much easier to make a correct program efficient than it is to make an efficient program correct.

---

[1] Try this for yourself and see: Find a friend who has an efficient program of which he is particularly proud. Draw your own conclusions about the ease with which the program can be understood.

A second conclusion: If you must optimize your program, do it in an organized, methodical way. Many programmers waste hours of computer time while they try to make a ten-microsecond procedure run in nine microseconds.

In the next section, we'll discuss a strategy for optimizing programs. Then, we can discuss the actual mechanics of making a program more efficient.

15.2 Strategy for optimization

Many programmers approach program optimization in a disorganized, helter-skelter fashion. This section details a systematic, step-by-step procedure that you should follow when optimizing your program.

First, make sure that your program works! A relatively inefficient program that produces correct output is generally tolerable, at least for the few days that it might take you to optimize the program. An efficient program that produces incorrect output is of little use to anyone.

Second, find out whether anyone cares about the possible inefficiency in your program. It's not unusual for a programmer to feel guilty about wasting three milliseconds of CPU time in a program that requires a *total* of only three seconds, and that executes only once a month in production! If your program runs daily, taking 26 hours of computer time, *then* start worrying!

Third, find out which part of your program is the most inefficient. This is particularly important, since it almost always will turn out that any inefficiencies are localized in a small part of your program. A number of studies have shown that 50 percent of the CPU time of a program typically is consumed by 5 percent of the code. In one real-time system involving roughly 300,000 instructions, approximately 1.5 percent of the code consumes 75 percent of the CPU time!

Unfortunately, most programmers are notoriously poor at *guessing* where the inefficiencies, or "hot spots," are concentrated. Too often, the programmer assumes that the module that was most difficult for him to code also will turn out to be the most inefficient. For all but the most trivial programs, we need some precise way of *measuring* CPU time, memory, disk accesses, and other resource requirements of a program. We will discuss this in more detail in Section 15.3 below.

Fourth, try to estimate how much of an improvement you can make in each module of your program, and roughly how long it will take to make that improvement. Even though you generally will want to optimize the module that is least efficient, a more useful guideline to follow is: *Optimize the module that will produce the largest gain in efficiency for the least cost.* If your program is still too inefficient, then optimize the module that will produce the next largest net improvement in efficiency for the least amount of work, and so forth.

Fifth, make use of any available optimizing compilers and optimizing packages to get cheap improvements in efficiency. These packages generally are hardware-dependent and vendor-dependent, so we will not discuss them here. However, you should check to see if such facilities are available in your organization. It is common for optimizing compilers to produce improvements of 10-20 percent in the efficiency of a program. However, the packages themselves consume considerable memory and CPU time, so they should be used only *after* your program has been debugged.

Sixth, once you have decided which module should be optimized, try to find a better *algorithm* for the module before you resort to clever coding tricks of the sort discussed in Section 15.4. For example, you may find that you have organized your file in a *sequential* fashion, even though you access only 100 records out of a file of 100,000 records. By making the file a *direct* file and accessing only those records required, you may be able to save hours of computer time.

Finally, if you *do* decide to recode a module to make it more efficient, insert copious comments indicating what you've done and why; otherwise, your program may be unintelligible.

15.3 Measuring the inefficiency in your program

As we have pointed out, most programmers are notoriously poor at guessing *where* their program consumes the bulk of its resources. Some organized method of *performance measurement* is usually necessary to avoid making the optimization process an entirely hit-or-miss affair.

Listed below are three basic approaches for measuring performance:

1. Use counters to count the number of times "interesting" events have occurred — for example, count the number of file accesses made, the number of times a table was searched for a particular entry, and, most important, *the number of times selected portions of code have been executed.*

2. Use the computer's real-time clock to measure the elapsed time between one portion of code and another.

3. Use a vendor-supplied package to capture the statistics automatically.

The first method is often satisfactory for taking crude measurements of the behavior of a program. For example, you might decide to count the number of times each paragraph in your program is executed. If there are, say, 100 paragraphs in the program, then you would define a 100-entry table in your DATA DIVISION, with each entry initialized to zero. Then you would add one statement to the beginning of each paragraph. For example:

```
    EDIT-CUSTOMER-RECORD.
*
* NOTE: THIS IS THE 17TH PARAGRAPH IN THE PROGRAM
*
    ADD 1 TO PARAGRAPH-COUNTER (17).
    .
    .
    .
```

Just prior to terminating the program, you would print the contents of the table.

While this approach is satisfactory for some simple applications, it has some obvious drawbacks. The primary limitation is that it doesn't tell us how much memory or CPU time is consumed by each paragraph. A somewhat less serious (although often *extremely* annoying) problem is that it requires a lot of tedious work to insert the measurement code, and to eventually remove it. This problem can be alleviated to some extent if you have a *pre-compiler* available. If not, we recommend that you introduce the code and then use a simple flag (whose value can be changed by recompiling the program) to determine whether the statistics actually should be printed.

There is one final disadvantage of the counter approach: The measurement code itself consumes some memory, CPU time, and I/O operations. Thus, it will slow your program and add some extra memory requirements.

The second approach — reading the real-time clock — is more precise, but it involves facilities that are not part of the standard COBOL language. Depending on the type of computer system you use, you may find that you can use the Job Control Language to request the operating system to measure the CPU time of an individual program. This may be a suitable approach if you have separately compiled CALLable subprograms. Alternatively, you may have to CALL an assembly language subroutine, which in turn will call the operating system to read the real-time clock. Inquire about how this operation is accomplished in your installation.

Assuming that you are able to gain access to the real-time clock, you may decide to measure the CPU time consumed by a COBOL section or paragraph, or possibly by even a single COBOL statement. In most cases, you'll want to keep track of the total number of times a unit of code is invoked, as well as the *total* CPU time consumed. From this, you can compute (manually or in a program) the average amount of CPU time required for each unit of code.

This technique for performance measurement has two disadvantages in common with the previous approach: You must modify your code in order to gather the statistics; and you do consume some additional overhead with the performance measurement logic. Even worse, the overhead is *included* with the measurements of your program — that is, if your statistics indicate that your program consumed 100 seconds of CPU time, you can expect that two to three seconds were involved in just *capturing* the statistics. Fortunately, the overhead tends to be relatively small, so you should be able to ignore it.

There is one other practical way to gather performance statistics about your program: Use a vendor-supplied package, if one is available in your EDP organization. Although it is beyond the scope of this book to describe how the variety of available hardware and software monitors work, you should be aware that they exist. Almost all such packages have the advantages that (a) they require little or no modification of your source program, and (b) they add little or no measurable overhead to the CPU time, memory, or other resource requirements of your program.

So, if you have access to a performance measurement package, it's probably the best way to obtain accurate, detailed information about your program. Otherwise, you should use the real-time clock to get accurate measurements of the execution speed of your program, and you should use strategically placed counters to obtain other useful information.

15.4 Programming techniques for efficiency

For every model of computer hardware, operating system, and programming language, there is a list of special tricks that can be used to save a microsecond of CPU time, a byte of memory, or a block of disk storage. While these tricks may be very important from time to time in your efforts to optimize your program, we will make no attempt to describe them in this book. Even if we could capture the thousands of programming tricks on various computers, they would be outdated by the time you read this book.

What we *can* do is discuss five of the most *common* programming techniques that can be used with virtually any version of COBOL to save memory and CPU time. These techniques are detailed in the following subsections.

15.4.1 Avoid Unnecessary Internal Data Conversions

One of the most common causes of inefficiency in a COBOL program is the unnecessary conversion of data from one format to another. As we have pointed out, COBOL expects data fields to be in certain formats in order to carry out certain operations. If the data are *not* in the required format, COBOL automatically will cause the data to be converted *when the program executes*. This conversion process involves some assembly language instructions that add extra memory requirements to the program, as well as slow it down.

For example, COBOL expects to carry out arithmetic operations (ADD, SUBTRACT, and so forth) on packed decimal fields — i.e., fields that have been defined as COMP or COMP-3. Thus, if you have defined a numeric field as

01 BALANCE-DUE   PIC 9(5)V99.

you can expect that a certain amount of inefficiency will result from any arithmetic operations on the field. COBOL will have to convert BALANCE-DUE from the DISPLAY format shown above to a packed decimal format for arithmetic operations, and then convert the result from a packed decimal format back into DISPLAY format.

It also is more efficient to define a numeric field as *signed* if your program is going to store data in the field; otherwise, COBOL will carry out specified computations on the field and then compute the *absolute magnitude* of the result to ensure that it is a positive number.

On most computers, it is also more efficient to specify an *odd* number of digits for a signed numeric field. This is because most computers require that a numeric field occupy an *even* number of positions in memory, and that the sign itself occupy one position. If you specify an *even* number of digits for your field, the COBOL compiler will generate instructions which will cause your program, *when it runs,* to (a) move the field to a temporary field that is defined with an odd number of digits, (b) carry out the arithmetic operations on the temporary field, and (c) move the results back into your field.

Another common internal data conversion involves *subscripts.* Since a subscript is used to compute the hardware address of an entry in a table, and since hardware memory locations have *binary* addresses, it follows that subscripts must be defined as a *binary* field.

15.4.2 Organize Searches Efficiently

As we stated in Chapter 11, COBOL provides two statements — SEARCH and SEARCH ALL — to look for entries in a table. With the SEARCH statement, an average of N/2 inspections is required to locate an entry in the table; with the SEARCH ALL statement, an average of $\log_2 N$ inspections is required. Thus, for a table with more than four entries, the binary search will generally require fewer inspections.

However, the binary search requires more overhead than the sequential search. Prior to each inspection of the table, the SEARCH ALL statement requires a computation to determine *which* table entry should be inspected next; with the SEARCH statement, COBOL merely has to increment a subscript by 1 to determine which entry should be inspected next. Because of this additional overhead, we usually find that it is not worth the bother of using a SEARCH ALL statement unless your table is 50-100 entries long (remember that the SEARCH ALL statement requires the table to be ordered, whereas SEARCH does not).

If you are using the SEARCH statement, and if the entries in your table do not change during execution of the program, there may be another opportunity to improve the efficiency of the SEARCH. Remember, an average of N/2 inspections will be required if *each* table entry has an equal probability of being selected. But in many real-world applications, that is not a reasonable assumption: You may find that 90 percent of all SEARCH statements are looking for one or two specific table entries.

Therefore, you should order the entries in the table so that the most popular entries appear first, and the least popular entries appear last. With this approach, you may find that the SEARCH statement requires only a couple of inspections instead of N/2 inspections.

With larger tables (e.g., tables that are several thousand entries long), you may need more sophisticated searching techniques than are available with the SEARCH and SEARCH ALL statements.[2] One commonly used technique is called a *hash-code,* or "randomizing," search. Its basic objective is to determine a *probable* table entry where the desired item will be found; when it works properly, the hash-code search will retrieve entries in an average of about 1.5 inspections of the table.

To illustrate the hash-code search, let's imagine that we have to maintain a table of the Social Security numbers of some 1,000 people in our organization. We could use a sequential search, but that would be unreasonably slow; even a binary search would require an average of ten inspections of the table before retrieving the desired Social Security number. The hash-code approach would involve (a) using a table of 1,000 entries to store the 1,000 Social Security numbers, (b) using an algorithm to determine where each employee record should be stored in the table, and (c) using the same algorithm to retrieve items from the table.

---

[2]For the numerous variations on the SEARCH mechanism, see Donald Knuth, *The Art of Computer Programming — Volume 3: Searching and Sorting* (Reading, Mass.: Addison-Wesley, 1973).

One simple algorithm for this example would be to divide an employee's Social Security number by the length of the table, and use the *remainder* as a subscript. Thus, an employee with Social Security number 130-34-9025 would be stored in table entry 025, while someone with Social Security number 093-44-7732 would be stored in table entry 732.

But what do we do with someone whose Social Security number is 130-34-5025? Such a situation is called a *collision,* or *overflow.* One reasonable approach would be to try putting Social Security number 130-34-5025 into table entry 026, since table entry 025 is already occupied by Social Security number 130-34-9025. Of course, we run the risk that table entry 026 is occupied, too — in which case, we could then examine entry 027. In other words, we use an algorithm to compute a probable *first* entry to examine; a sequential search (which may have to wrap around the end of the table) is used thereafter. If the distribution of employee numbers is reasonably random, our hashcode search will be very efficient; if it turns out that *all* employees have a Social Security number ending in 025, the search will degenerate into a pure sequential search (in which case, we should choose another algorithm!).

15.4.3 Organize IF-ELSE-IF Constructs Efficiently

Consider the following sequence of code:

```
IF MARITAL-STATUS = 'DIVORCED'
    PERFORM DIVORCED-ROUTINE
ELSE IF MARITAL-STATUS = 'SEPARATED'
    PERFORM SEPARATED-ROUTINE
ELSE IF MARITAL-STATUS = 'SINGLE'
    PERFORM SINGLE-ROUTINE
ELSE IF MARITAL-STATUS = 'MARRIED'
    PERFORM MARRIED-ROUTINE
ELSE
    PERFORM BAD-MARITAL-STATUS.
```

What if it turns out that 80 percent of the cases we deal with involve a marital status of married, and only 5 percent of the cases we deal with are divorced or separated? Obviously, our program wastes some time before discovering the most likely cases. To make our program more efficient, we should reorganize the sequence of tests so that the most likely conditions will be discovered first.

Of course, the programmer may have had no idea when he wrote this program which case would be most likely — and, as we pointed out in Section 15.1, he should not worry about it then. *After* the program is working, appropriate performance measurement techniques can determine whether this sequence of tests constitutes a serious inefficiency in the program, and which marital status is the most common.

15.4.4 Arrange Blocking and Buffering for Efficiency

As we discussed in Chapter 12, you can specify with the RESERVE *n* ALTERNATE AREAS whether each of your files will have one buffer, two buffers, or *n* buffers. Your program generally will require *more* memory and *less* CPU time if you specify a large number of buffers; conversely, it will require *less* memory and *more* CPU time if you specify only one buffer.

In most cases, a point of diminishing returns is reached after your program is given three or four buffers. If it takes your program significantly longer to process one record than it takes the operating system to bring the next record into memory, then it is pointless to have more than two buffers — the operating system will always be able to overlap its input operation with your program's computing. Similarly, if it takes *much* longer for the operating system to bring the next record into memory than it takes your program to process the record, then it won't help to have 200 buffers. Your program still will get ahead of the operating system, and be forced to wait while the next record is brought into memory. However, it may turn out that your program processes five to ten records very quickly and then spends a considerably longer period of time processing the next record (this is common in sequential file processing, where many records can be examined quickly and then written to the output file, while a relatively small number of records require lengthy processing). In such a case, additional buffers can make the program run much faster.

Similarly, *blocking factors* can be adjusted to make a program more efficient. By making the blocking factor small, we have small physical records and thereby conserve memory. On the other hand, we make *less* efficient use of the storage space on the I/O device, and we incur more physical I/O operations, which will make our program run more slowly. Conversely, a large blocking factor will require more memory (since each physical block read by the operating system will contain more logical records), but will make better use of the physical I/O device and generally will allow our program to run faster.

15.4.5 Change CALL Statements to PERFORM Statements

In some cases, you may find that your program operates inefficiently because of the overhead of the CALL statement and its associated passing of data through the LINKAGE SECTION. This usually will be localized to one or two CALLable subprograms that are invoked frequently. If a module is invoked only a few times, the inefficiency of the CALL statement can usually be disregarded.

There is a disadvantage to replacing CALLs with PERFORMs: Doing so means that all of the modules will share the same DATA DIVISION, thereby increasing the chance that a bug in module A will cause some of module B's data to be mysteriously destroyed. So, it's best to avoid this type of optimization if you possibly can — if you *must* do it, change only those modules that are invoked a substantial number of times.

On occasion, you may even find that the PERFORM statement slows your program more than you can afford. Or, on a virtual memory system, you may find that the module that executes the PERFORM statement is on a different page than the module being PERFORMed. In such cases, it may make sense to code the PERFORMed module *in-line* in the module which invokes it. If the PERFORMed module was invoked from two or three superordinates, use the COPY statement to place an exact copy of the module in-line. Naturally, two or three copies of a module will add memory requirements to your program. However, it generally will make the program run faster, and it may eliminate some nasty thrashing in a virtual memory environment.

AFTERWORD

The purpose of this book has been to make you a productive COBOL programmer, not an expert on every aspect of the language. To become an expert, you would have to memorize the COBOL reference manual, and no one expects that. An excellent programmer knows where to find answers, but does not have to know *all* the answers. As with the programmers before you, your training has just begun, and it will continue until you retire from the profession. The problems we solve are constantly evolving, and the tools we use are changing with them.

We hope that this book has given you a good start, but now we encourage you to continue your education. A COBOL reference manual is a necessary text, and other programmers' code is an endless source of practical information on style and technique. We also recommend that you become a regular reader of at least one of the data processing periodicals. They are heralds of the future, and forums for the problems of the present.

We welcome you to programming. Work, learn, and enjoy!

References to *Learning to Program in Structured COBOL, Part 1* have been tossed about glibly throughout this text . . . but it occurs to us that some few of you may have never been exposed to *Part 1* and that your curiosity as to the actual contents may have been sufficiently piqued. We, therefore, offer you the following abstract of the Table of Contents for *Learning to Program in Structured COBOL, Part 1:*

CONTENTS

APPENDIX

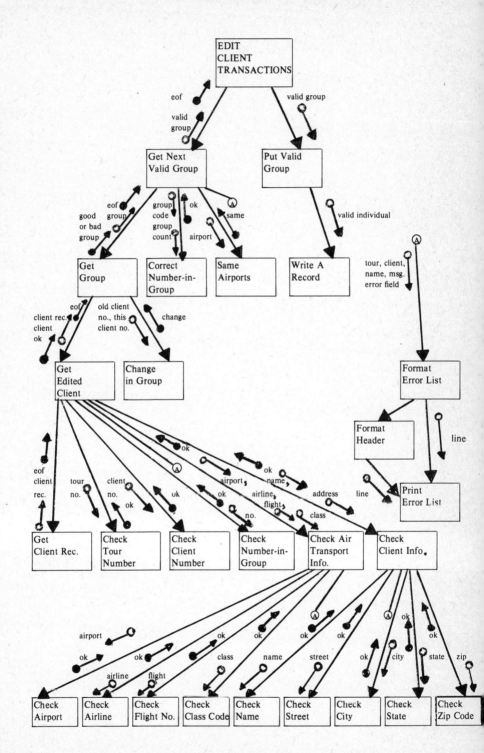

W&P sample flowchart.

1.   TALLY = 4, FIELD = **bbbb**4

2.   TALLY = UNCHANGED, FIELD = BENENE

3.   NUMB-COUNT = 4, FIELD = **bb**1346

4.   TALLY = UNCHANGED, FIELD = QDAMENT

1)   +24.6

2)   −6.7

3)   +2,468

4)   +22

5)   + 1

6)   − 6

7)   16+

8)   22.060−

9)   .01−

A note about Problems 5 and 6: With only one occurrence of the "+" in the editing PIC, the "+" is interpreted as fixed in position, regardless of whether leading zeroes are suppressed by Z characters.

```
IDENTIFICATION DIVISION.
PROGRAM-ID. FORMATDL.
ENVIRONMENT DIVISION.
DATA DIVISION.
WORKING-STORAGE SECTION.
*
*
01  PRINT-LINE.
    05  FILLER                      PIC X(5).
    05  PR-TOUR-NUM                 PIC 99-999/9.
    05  FILLER                      PIC X(5).
    05  PR-AGT-CLIENT               PIC 99-999-9.
    05  IND-CLIENT REDEFINES PR-AGT-CLIENT.
        10  PR-IND-CLIENT           PIC 9-99999.
        10  FILLER                  PIC X.
    05  FILLER                      PIC X(5).
    05  PR-CLIENT-NAME              PIC X(30).
    05  FILLER                      PIC X(5).
    05  PR-NUMBER-GROUP             PIC Z9.
    05  FILLER                      PIC X(5).
    05  PR-TOTAL-COST               PIC $$$$,$$9.99.
    05  FILLER                      PIC X(5).
    05  PR-DEPOSIT                  PIC $$$$,$$9.99
    05  FILLER                      PIC X(5).
    05  PR-BAL-DUE                  PIC $$$$,$$9.99CR.
    05  FILLER                      PIC X(5).
    05  PR-DEPART-DATE              PIC 99/99/99.
    05  FILLER                      PIC X.
*
01  WS-TOTAL-COST                   PIC S9(6)V99.
01  WS-BAL-DUE                      PIC S9(6)V99.
01  WS-DEPART-DATE.
    05  WS-MONTH-DAY                PIC 9(4).
    05  WS-YEAR                     PIC 99.
*
*
*
LINKAGE SECTION.
*
01  CLIENT-RECD.
    05  CLIENT-NUMBER               PIC 9(6).
    05  IND-OR-AGT                  PIC A.
        88  INDEPEND                VALUE 'I'.
        88  AGENCY                  VALUE 'A'.
    05  TOUR-NUMBER                 PIC 9(6).
    05  CLIENT-NAME                 PIC X(30).
```

```
    05  NUM-IN-GROUP              PIC 99.
    05  COST-FOR-ONE             PIC S9(4)V99.
    05  DEPOSIT                  PIC S9(6)V99.
    05  DATE-DEPART.
        10  DEPART-YEAR          PIC 99.
        10  DEPART-MONTH-DAY     PIC 9(4).
    05  FILLER                   PIC X(15).
*
*

PROCEDURE DIVISION
    USING CLIENT-RECD.
*****
* FORMATDL FORMATS A DETAIL-LINE, NAMED PRINT-LINE
* AND THEN CALLS PRINTDL TO PRINT IT.  FORMATDL
* IS CALLED BY BILL REPT.
*****
FORMAT-RECD.
    MULTIPLY COST-FOR-ONE BY NUM-IN-GROUP
        GIVING WS-TOTAL-COST.
    SUBTRACT DEPOSIT FROM WS-TOTAL-COST
        GIVING WS-BAL-DUE.
    MOVE DEPART-MONTH-DAY TO WS-MONTH-DAY.
    MOVE DEPART-YEAR TO WS-YEAR.
*
*

    MOVE SPACES TO PRINT-LINE.
    MOVE TOUR-NUMBER TO PR-TOUR-NUM.
    IF INDEPEND
        MOVE CLIENT-NUMBER TO PR-IND-CLIENT
    ELSE
        MOVE CLIENT-NUMBER TO PR-AGT-CLIENT.
    MOVE CLIENT-NAME TO PR-CLIENT-NAME.
    MOVE NUM-IN-GROUP TO PR-NUMBER-GROUP.
    MOVE WS-TOTAL-COST TO PR-TOTAL-COST.
    MOVE DEPOSIT TO PR-DEPOSIT.
    MOVE WS-BAL-DUE TO PR-BAL-DUE.
    MOVE WS-DEPART-DATE TO PR-DEPART-DATE.
*
*

    CALL 'PRINTDL' USING PRINT-LINE.
*
*

EXIT-FORMATDL.
    EXIT PROGRAM.
```

WORKING-STORAGE SECTION.
01 BOOK-VALUES.
```
        05   FILLER                    PIC 9(2)         VALUE 01.
        05   FILLER                    PIC S9(2)V99     VALUE +09.95.
        05   FILLER                    PIC S9(2)V99     VALUE +08.95.
        05   FILLER                    PIC S9(2)V99     VALUE +07.00
        05   FILLER                    PIC 9(2)         VALUE 02.
        05   FILLER                    PIC S9(2)V99     VALUE +16.50.
        05   FILLER                    PIC S9(2)V99     VALUE +14.00.
        05   FILLER                    PIC S9(2)V99     VALUE +12.00.
        05   FILLER                    PIC 9(2)         VALUE 03.
        05   FILLER                    PIC S9(2)V99     VALUE +34.49.
        05   FILLER                    PIC S9(2)V99     VALUE +32.49.
        05   FILLER                    PIC S9(2)V99     VALUE +28.00.
        05   FILLER                    PIC 9(2)         VALUE 04.
        05   FILLER                    PIC S9(2)V99     VALUE +07.75.
        05   FILLER                    PIC S9(2)V99     VALUE +07.25.
        05   FILLER                    PIC S9(2)V99     VALUE +06.25.
        05   FILLER                    PIC 9(2)         VALUE 05.
        05   FILLER                    PIC S9(2)V99     VALUE +12.50.
        05   FILLER                    PIC S9(2)V99     VALUE +11.50.
        05   FILLER                    PIC S9(2)V99     VALUE +10.50.
        05   FILLER                    PIC 9(2)         VALUE 06.
        05   FILLER                    PIC S9(2)V99     VALUE +03.50.
        05   FILLER                    PIC S9(2)V99     VALUE +03.50.
        05   FILLER                    PIC S9(2)V99     VALUE +03.50.
        05   FILLER                    PIC 9(2)         VALUE 07.
        05   FILLER                    PIC S9(2)V99     VALUE +19.95.
        05   FILLER                    PIC S9(2)V99     VALUE +18.50.
        05   FILLER                    PIC S9(2)V99     VALUE +17.00.
        05   FILLER                    PIC 9(2)         VALUE 08.
        05   FILLER                    PIC S9(2)V99     VALUE +04.00.
        05   FILLER                    PIC S9(2)V99     VALUE +03.50.
        05   FILLER                    PIC S9(2)V99     VALUE +02.95.

01   BOOK-TABLE REDEFINES BOOK-VALUES.
        05   BOOK-ENTRY OCCURS 8 TIMES INDEXED BY THIS-BOOK.
             10   BOOK-CODE-TB          PIC 9(2).
             10   MAX-PRICE             PIC S9(2)V99.
             10   SMALL-DISC-PRICE      PIC S9(2)V99.
             10   BIG-DISC-PRICE        PIC S9(2)V99.
```

```
01  MIN-FOR-SMALL-DISC       PIC 9(2)      VALUE 06.
01  MIN-FOR-BIG-DISC         PIC 9(2)      VALUE 12.
01  NUMBER-OF-BOOKS          PIC 9         VALUE 8.

LINKAGE SECTION.
01  BOOK-CODE-LK             PIC 9(2).
01  NUMBER-ORDERED           PIC 9(2).
01  AMT-DUE                  PIC S9(4)V99.

PROCEDURE DIVISION
    USING                    BOOK-CODE-LK
                             NUMBER-ORDERED
                             AMT-DUE.

CALC-AMT-DUE.
    PERFORM MATCH-CODES
        VARYING THIS-BOOK FROM 1 BY 1
        UNTIL BOOK-CODE-TB (THIS-BOOK) = BOOK-CODE-LK
            OR THIS-BOOK GREATER THAN NUMBER-OF-BOOKS.

    IF THIS-BOOK GREATER THAN NUMBER-OF-BOOKS
        MOVE ZEROES TO AMT-DUE
    ELSE IF NUMBER-ORDERED LESS THAN MIN-FOR-SMALL-DISC
        MULTIPLY NUMBER-ORDERED BY MAX-PRICE (THIS-BOOK)
            GIVING AMT-DUE
    ELSE IF NUMBER-ORDERED LESS THAN MIN-FOR-BIG-DISC
        MULTIPLY NUMBER-ORDERED BY SMALL-DISC-PRICE (THIS-BOOK)
            GIVING AMT-DUE
    ELSE
        MULTIPLY NUMBER-ORDERED BY BIG-DISC-PRICE (THIS-BOOK)
            GIVING AMT-DUE.
EXIT-AMT-CALC.
    EXIT PROGRAM.

MATCH-CODES.
    EXIT.
*
* THIS PARAGRAPH IS A DUMMY BECAUSE THE PERFORM-VARYING HANDLES
* THE ENTIRE TABLE LOOKUP.
*
```

GLOSSARY

abend
an acronym for "abnormal end"; used on many IBM computers to describe a situation that causes a computer program to terminate its execution abnormally.

ANSI
an abbreviation for American National Standards Institute, the organization which (among other things) establishes the standard definition of the COBOL language.

asynchronous execution
a way of organizing two or more processes (in the context of this book, the operating system and a COBOL program) so that each can execute independently of the other, except for occasional references made by one process to the other to check on completion of an event, or to check on progress, or otherwise to *synchronize* its activities with those of the other process.

binary search

a strategy of searching through tables that, after each inspection of the table, reduces the number of remaining entries to be searched by half. Also known as a *logarithmic search,* since the average number of inspections to find a specified entry in the table is $\log_2 N$, where N is the length of the table.

binding

a synonym for *cohesion.*

black box

a common description of a system whose inputs, outputs, and function are known, but whose inner workings are unknown and irrelevant.

blocking

the process of combining several *logical records* into one *physical record.*

blocking factor

an integer which describes the number of *logical records* that have been placed in one *physical record.*

bubble chart

a synonym for *program graph.*

buffer

an area of memory into which the operating system reads records from an input-output device,

	or from which the operating system writes records onto an input-output device.
buffering	the process of providing more than one buffer in a program, so that the operating system can *asynchronously* read records into or write records from one buffer while the COBOL program uses the data in another buffer.
central transforms	those *bubbles* in a *program graph* that are involved in computing, or transforming the inputs to the program into the outputs of the program.
cohesion	a measure of the relatedness of elements (e.g., instructions or subordinate modules) of a COBOL module.
collision	a phenomenon that occurs when a *hash-code search* computes the same probable table entry for two unique data elements.
coupling	a measure of the interconnections between COBOL modules.

data exception | an informal, but common term to describe an *abend* caused by a program's attempt to manipulate data that is in a form other than that defined in the PIC clause.

debugging | the process of identifying the location, cause, and cure for a bug, once the existence of the bug has been made known.

direct access | a method of organizing files, so that the program can access a desired record directly without having to read and discard all of the records which precede the desired record. Usually contrasted with *sequential access*.

EBCDIC | an acronym for Extended Binary Coded Decimal Interchange Code. One of several conventions for representing the set of printable characters as binary codes.

functional cohesion | the strongest form of *cohesion*. A module with functional cohesion contains elements (for example, instructions or subordinate modules) which are necessary and sufficient to carry out one single, well-defined task.

hash-code search

a searching algorithm in which the desired table entry is used to compute a probable index in the table. The algorithm used to compute the probable address is used both to store entries in the table and to retrieve entries from the table.

in-line code

a synonym for *lexically included code*.

incremental testing

a testing strategy in which one untested (and potentially bug-ridden) module is added to a set of previously tested modules. The process is repeated until all modules have been tested.

interrecord gap

an area between two *physical records* on an input-output device (typically, magnetic tape or disk). Used by the computer hardware to detect the end of one record and the beginning of another record.

intermediate file

a file produced as output by one program, and

used as input in another program, but which is not saved for any other purpose after the programs have finished executing.

JCL

an abbreviation for *Job Control Language.*

Job Control Language

an informal term used to describe the instructions by which a programmer tells the operating system how the program should be executed — e.g., how much memory the program requires, what priority it should have, what names have been given to the physical files, and so forth.

lexically included code

COBOL statements that have been identified on a structure chart as distinct, cohesive module(s), but which are coded within the body of the next higher-level superordinate module(s).

logical cohesion

one of the weaker levels of *cohesion.* A logically cohesive module contains processing elements (for example, statements or subordinate modules) that perform a variety of similar tasks, but do not perform   one   single, well-defined task.

logical record

a data record as seen by the computer programmer, and as defined in the COBOL program. Usually contrasted with *physical record*.

memory dump

a debugging strategy in which the contents of all or part of the computer's memory is printed, often in almost unreadable form.

merging

the process of combining the records in two or more files, to produce a single file whose records are ordered.

multidimensional table

a table with two or more distinct subscripts.

packed decimal

a form of data representation that permits two decimal digits to be stored in one byte of computer memory.

physical record

a record of data, as stored on an input-output device. A physical record contains one or more *logical records*.

program graph

a diagram that shows the flow of data elements through a program, and the transformations of data from one form to another form.

pseudocode

a means of describing procedural logic by using imperative English statements, IF-THEN-ELSE constructs, and DO-WHILE constructs. Also known as structured English, or program design language.

recording density

a measure of the amount of data that can be stored on one unit (e.g., a block or a track) of a physical input/output device.

sequential access

a method of accessing records from a file in which the Nth record may be obtained only by first reading the first N-1 records of the file. Usually contrasted with *direct access*.

sorting

the process of rearranging the records of a file so that they appear in sequential order.

structure chart

a form of program documentation that shows the modules of a COBOL program, and the connections between modules.

stub · a module that provides a primitive simulation of a subordinate module during the testing of a superordinate module. Normally used as part of a process of *top-down testing.*

subordinate module · a module that is CALLed or PERFORMed by some other module, that is, one that is hierarchically lower than some other module.

superordinate module · a module that CALLs or PERFORMs some other module, i.e., one that is hierarchically higher than some other module.

top-down testing · a testing strategy in which higher-level modules are tested first (usually by supplying *stubs* for the subordinate modules), and lower-level modules are tested last. Usually associated with *incremental testing.*

transform analysis · a design strategy that derives a *structure chart* for a program by analyzing the *program graph* for the problem.

transform-centered design · a synonym for *transform analysis.*

INDEX